the world in *bite* size

PAUL GAYLER

the world in *bite* size

tapas, mezze, and other tasty morsels

photography by Peter Cassidy

Kyle Books

To Anita, with love

This edition published in 2008 by Kyle Books   An imprint of Kyle Cathie Limited   www.kylecathie.com

Distributed by National Book Network, 4501 Forbes Blvd., Suite 200, Lanham, MD 20706 Phone: (301) 459 3366 Fax: (301) 429 5746

Text © 2007 Paul Gayler Photography © 2007 Peter Cassidy Book design © 2007 Kyle Cathie Limited

First published in Great Britain in 2007 by Kyle Cathie Limited www.kylecathie.com

ISBN 978-1-904920-72-4
10 9 8 7 6 5 4 3 2

Library of Congress Control Number: 2007939787

Project editor Jennifer Wheatley **Designer** Jane Humphrey **Photographer** Peter Cassidy (see also page 192) **Home economist** Linda Tubby **Styling** Róisín Nield (apart from pages 20, 27, 41, 58, 103, 148–151, 183; Helen Trent) **Copy editor** Emily Hatchwell **Americanizer** Delora Jones **Production** Sha Huxtable and Alice Holloway

Recipe photographs refer to the first recipe featured on the facing page

small eating is becoming a big deal.

No longer do we have to sit down to a three-course meal whenever we eat out. Instead, more and more restaurants are offering a menu of "small plates," from which we can mix and match as we please.

Little bites of food amuse, stimulate, and excite the palate. They give both the cook and the diner an opportunity to experiment with a variety of different ingredients, and there is always something to suit everyone's taste—perfect for people who can never make up their mind!

The phenomenon of bite-size eating isn't new. It has its roots in some of the world's greatest cuisines: think of the tapas of Spain, the antipasti of Italy, the dim sum of China, the tiffin of India, and the mezze of the Middle East. What is new, however, is that these little dishes are now becoming the main event, rather than just something to awaken the appetite before a meal. For diners, it's a relaxed and sociable way of eating. For chefs, it's an inspiring way to cook—an opportunity to play around with tastes, textures, and flavors without being constrained by the conventions of the three-course meal.

Bite-size eating was born out of Spanish tapas, which are thought to have originated in Andalucía several hundred years ago. A piece of bread or cured meat, or some olives or nuts, was placed on a saucer on top of glasses to stop flies from getting in the drink (the word *tapar* means "to cover"). This evolved to include more elaborate dishes, such as tortilla (potato omelette), *patatas bravas* (fried potatoes with a spicy tomato sauce), and grilled shellfish and sausages. It's customary in Spain to move from one bar to another sampling the different fare, which is always accompanied by a glass of wine or sherry. A similar ritual takes place in Venice, where bar snacks known as *cicchetti* are eaten with a glass of wine between meals. It's a sociable ritual, where meeting up with friends and chatting about the events of the day are the priority, and little plates of food help to assuage hunger and temper the effects of alcohol.

Perhaps the Mediterranean climate encourages this kind of eating. When the sun's beating down it's more tempting to nibble at an assortment of little dishes than to embark on a big meal. The countries of the Eastern Mediterranean have their own version of "small-plate" eating, in the form of mezze. Laden with fragrantly spiced little dishes, the mezze table is an awesome sight: smooth, creamy purees such as hummus, taramasalata, and baba ghanoush; elegant pastries such as *spanokopita*, filled with meat, vegetables, or cheese; rustic salads and smoky grilled vegetables; crisp fritters of seafood or fish, served with little sauces for dipping—all garnished with fresh herbs and enlivened with the warm, aromatic spices of the region. What was once intended to start a meal has become the main feature.

The Far East, too, has a long tradition of small bites. Street vendors throughout the region sell delicacies that can be held in the hand and are easy to eat. Then there's the great tradition of dim sum, originating in China's tea houses, where a feast of bite-size food is wheeled to your table on trolleys stacked high with bamboo baskets: buns stuffed with roast pork, translucent little dumplings filled with shrimp, spring rolls, little croquettes, steamed spare ribs, and much more. Dim sum has become hugely popular in the West, matched only by the craze for sushi. Once street food in Japan, eaten by the poor, sushi is now big business, and is so successful in the West that it has been described as "Japanese tapas." Conveyor-belt sushi restaurants, where tempting little morsels are prepared in front of your eyes and then moved slowly past you in a mesmerizing procession, are all the rage. Unlike the tapas bar with its convivial atmosphere, these restaurants can feel functional and canteen-like. But they feed the never-ending appetite for small plates, and for a new, informal, deconstructed way of eating.

how to serve bite-size food Small plates of food are a fantastic way to entertain at home, and perfectly suited to today's casual style of eating. A well thought-out selection of bite-size foods can easily replace a more traditional offering, whether you serve them for a sit-down meal or buffet style, with drinks. Sharing plates of food is a sociable, informal affair, and passing the plates around breaks down barriers and encourages conversation.

Here are a few points to bear in mind when planning a "bite-size" meal:

– Keep the dishes small—they look more tempting this way, and they are also easier to serve, either by fork or spoon, or by hand.

– Aim to achieve a mix of colors, tastes, and textures, so that all the dishes look as enticing as possible.

– Vary the cooking techniques, both to make things easier for yourself and to provide a pleasing selection for your guests—for example, a couple of dishes might be baked in the oven, a couple fried or grilled, and you could also serve some salads and breads.

– Stay true to one cuisine, so the meal has some coherence—don't mix Spanish tapas with dim sum, for example!

– Modern presentation can be a lot of fun, so be sure to use a range of unusual dishes, deep bowls, glasses, spoons, or skewers.

– Remember, you don't even have to cook at all. A simple tapas selection could consist of some good olives and salted almonds, piquillo peppers, an assortment of cured meats, a couple of cheeses, and some bread and salad.

– As with all simple things, good-quality ingredients are key.

In this book I have tried to create an exciting and varied selection of recipes. I hope it inspires you to experience for yourself the wonderful flavors that small-plate eating has to offer. There are simple dishes, quickly cooked on the grill or in a wok, some light, some more robust. Other dishes are more complex, but very rewarding. I have been careful to respect culinary traditions but occasionally I like to fuse flavors and techniques.

serving sizes The recipes are designed to serve four people an appetizer-size portion; if necessary, you can double the quantities to serve as a main dish.

the americas

Mexico has its *botanas*, Colombia its *pasabocas*, and Argentina its *picadas*—a long tradition of delicious bite-size snacks served in markets, bars, and cafés, enticing passers-by with their pungent aromas and bright, fresh colors.

9oz fresh crabmeat (excess water
  squeezed out)
½ teaspoon green Tabasco sauce
2 scallions finely chopped
1 teaspoon ground cumin
2 tablespoons freshly chopped cilantro
½ cup canned corn drained
²⁄₃ cup mashed potato
1 egg beaten
2¹⁄₃ cups panko (Japanese-style
  bread crumbs)
sea salt (or kosher salt) and freshly
  ground black pepper
virgin olive oil for frying
garlic mayonnaise for serving

louisiana crab hash

One of the highlights of traveling to America over the years has been visiting
the Deep South, with its mélange of cuisines. I created this dish based on a
Louisiana-style crabcake recipe. Simply dig in with a fork before everybody else
gets to it.

1 Place the crabmeat, Tabasco, scallions, cumin, cilantro, and corn in a bowl, mix
  well, and season to taste. Add the mashed potato, then the egg and the crumbs.
  Adjust the seasoning again and mix well.
2 Heat a small, shallow-sided omelette pan with a little olive oil. When hot, add
  the crab mixture, pressing it down to fill the bottom of the pan. Fry until golden,
  about 2–3 minutes, then crush it lightly, fold over the outside to the center,
  and fry again for another 2–3 minutes, until the mixture is slightly crusty in
  appearance.
3 Turn out the hash into a bowl and let it cool slightly before cutting it into
  wedges. Serve with the garlic mayonnaise.

pg tip Japanese-style bread crumbs, or panko, are coarse in texture and
beautifully light and crisp when fried. They are available in good supermarkets
and Oriental grocery stores, but you can make your own version at home.
Spread some coarse white bread crumbs in a baking tray and bake in the
oven, at 325°F, stirring often, until they are crisp but not brown. This takes
8–10 minutes.

2 tablespoons buttermilk (or milk)

1 large egg white *lightly beaten until foamy*

¼ teaspoon garlic salt

⅛ teaspoon paprika

dash of Tabasco sauce

1 cup flour

½ teaspoon cayenne pepper

sea salt (or kosher salt) and freshly ground black pepper

10oz cooked crayfish tails or small shrimp *drained*

vegetable oil *for deep-frying*

cajun popcorn

If you can't find cooked crayfish tails in brine, small shrimp would also fit the bill nicely. The crispy crayfish cry out to be dunked in a spicy dip: try jazzing up a good-quality mayonnaise with a little Cajun spice, or tomato ketchup with a few drops of Tabasco.

1 In a bowl, combine the milk, egg, garlic salt, paprika, and Tabasco. Place the flour in another bowl and season with the cayenne, salt, and pepper.

2 Dip the crayfish tails in the milk mixture, then dredge them in the seasoned flour.

3 Heat the vegetable oil to 350°F, immerse the crayfish into the hot oil and fry until golden and crispy. Remove with a slotted spoon and drain on paper towels.

⅓ cup fine cornmeal

⅓ cup flour

1 teaspoon sugar

1 teaspoon baking powder

sea salt (or kosher salt) and freshly ground black pepper

1 egg *beaten*

½ cup milk

8 large hot dogs (or merguez if you prefer)

vegetable oil *for deep-frying*

mustard *for serving*

corn dogs

A corn dog is basically a hot dog coated in a cornmeal batter and deep-fried (though it can also be baked). Most corn dogs are served on wooden skewers nowadays, but the original one—apparently invented in Minnesota in 1941—presumably was not!

1 In a bowl, combine the cornmeal, flour, sugar, and baking powder, and season with salt and pepper. Beat in the egg and milk to form a batter, then let it stand for 30 minutes.

2 Spear each hot dog lengthwise with a soaked bamboo skewer, leaving enough skewer protruding for a handle.

3 Heat the vegetable oil in a deep pan to 300°F. Dip each hot dog into the batter and then immerse into the hot oil. Fry until golden and crispy, then remove with a slotted spoon. Drain on paper towels.

4 Serve with your favorite mustard.

1¼ cups orange juice

1 tablespoon hot pepper sauce

¾ cup white wine vinegar

3 garlic cloves *crushed*

1 tablespoon dried oregano

½ tablespoon cumin seeds

1 tablespoon annatto seeds (optional)

2 tablespoons vegetable oil

1lb 10oz pork belly *skinned and boned*

⅔ cup dark beer

8 flour tortillas

for the relish

¼ cup sugar

⅓ cup rice wine vinegar

2 red onions *very thinly sliced*

rolled pork burritos

Cooking pork in beer, peppers, and orange may sound unlikely, but believe me it really works. Make sure that after cooking the pork you bind it well in the reduced cooking juices, as this helps to keep the meat juicy and moist.

1 Preheat the oven to 350°F.

2 In a blender, mix together the orange juice, pepper sauce, vinegar, garlic, oregano, cumin, and annatto seeds (if using).

3 Heat the oil in a heavy, ovenproof pan, then add the pork and seal it all over. Pour the beer over it, along with the contents of the blender. Cover with a lid and place in the oven to braise for 1–1½ hours, or until the meat is very tender.

4 Meanwhile, make the relish. Boil the sugar and vinegar in a pan together for 2–3 minutes, then pour it over the onions in a bowl. Let them cool.

5 When the pork is cooked, lift it out into a large bowl and shred the meat with two forks. Meanwhile, place the orange sauce over a high heat, letting it reduce until thick enough to coat the meat.

6 Spoon the reduced sauce onto the shredded meat and mix to combine.

7 To serve, simply roll up the shredded pork in the tortillas, cut them in half, and top with the onion relish.

8 small chicken drumsticks
1 small onion *finely chopped*
1 red chile *seeded and finely chopped*
2 tablespoons Monterey Jack cheese
  (or sharp cheddar) *grated*
3oz merguez sausage (or fresh chorizo)
  very finely chopped
3 tablespoons virgin olive oil
8 slices bacon
sea salt (or kosher salt) and freshly
  ground black pepper
2 tablespoons honey
2 tablespoons dark soy sauce
freshly chopped cilantro *for serving*

tex-mex chicken

The spicy merguez sausage originates in North Africa, but it is used extensively in Latin cooking. I love it immensely. The smokiness of the sausage's chilli-pork base goes superbly with the chicken in this recipe.

1 Firstly, you need to bone the drumsticks. Starting with the knee joint, carefully separate the chicken meat from the bone with the tip of a small knife. Follow the bone up, keeping the flesh intact until you reach the top of the drumstick.

2 Roll back the flesh and, carefully, using a large chopping knife, cut off the bone about ½ inch from the top. This should give you a boned-out drumstick with just a small piece of bone protruding at one end. (A friendly butcher will do this if necessary!)

3 Mix the onion, chile, cheese, merguez and half the oil together in a bowl, then use this mixture to fill each drumstick cavity. Wrap each drumstick in a slice of bacon and then secure with a toothpick. Season liberally.

4 Heat a grill pan until hot. Brush the drumsticks with the remaining oil, place on the grill, and cook for 10–12 minutes.

5 Boil the honey and soy sauce together in a pan and brush this mixture liberally onto the chicken drumsticks as they cook. Serve sprinkled with the cilantro.

pg tip These chicken drumsticks are delicious served with a spicy tomato ketchup, made by simply adding a little creamed horseradish and a squeeze of lemon juice to regular tomato ketchup.

½ teaspoon Tabasco sauce

1 teaspoon Worcestershire sauce

1 teaspoon soy sauce

2 tablespoons chopped flat-leaf parsley

1 small red chile *finely chopped*

1 small onion *chopped*

1 teaspoon cayenne pepper

1 teaspoon garlic salt

18oz chicken wings

4 tablespoons tomato ketchup

for the dip

⅓ cup sour cream

½ cup blue cheese *crumbled*

buffalo hot wings

Chicken wings are eaten in many forms throughout the world, but for me the buffalo style takes a lot of beating—but then again I am a great spice lover.

1 Mix all the ingredients (except the chicken and the tomato ketchup) together in a bowl. Place the chicken wings in the marinade and marinate for 1 hour.

2 Preheat the oven to 350°F.

3 Transfer the contents of the bowl to a roasting pan and place in the oven for 30–35 minutes, turning the wings occasionally. When cooked, remove from the oven and let cool slightly.

4 Heat a grill pan until very hot, place the wings on the grill, and cook for another 5 minutes. Mix the tomato ketchup with a little of the cooking marinade and use this to baste the wings as they cook.

5 Mix together the sour cream and blue cheese and serve alongside the hot wings.

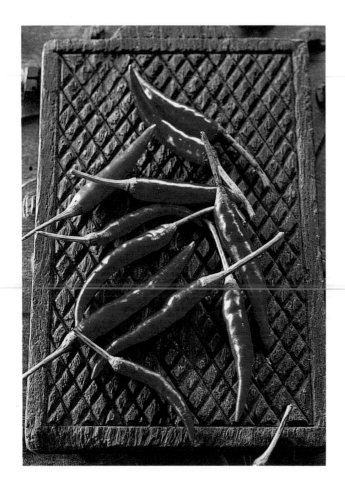

10oz Swiss chard *stalks removed*

2 tablespoons virgin olive oil

1 small onion *finely chopped*

2½ tablespoons fresh chorizo sausage (or another spicy sausage) *finely chopped*

14oz baby new potatoes *cooked and cut in half*

4oz sunblush or sundried tomatoes *roughly chopped*

½ cup Monterey Jack cheese (or sharp cheddar) *grated*

sea salt (or kosher salt)

spicy mexican potatoes

These are simply a variation of the Spanish *patatas bravas*.

1 Wash the Swiss chard and place in a pan with only the water that clings to the leaves. Cook for 5 minutes over a very low heat, then remove and let cool. Roughly chop the leaves.

2 Heat the olive oil in a large nonstick frying pan over a high heat. Add the onion and chorizo and fry until the onion is golden and the oil has been released from the chorizo.

3 Add the potatoes to the pan and fry until golden all over, taking care not to let the onion burn. Add the tomatoes and chopped chard, and cook all together for another 3–4 minutes, until the flavors are amalgamated. Add the cheese and remove from the heat immediately.

4 Season with a little salt, to taste, then serve.

pg tip Monterey Jack cheese, from California, is one of the few distinctively American cheeses; it is sometimes known simply as "Jack cheese." A mild cheese made from cow's milk, its consistency ranges from soft to hard, depending upon the cheese's maturity. It is often used in Latin dishes, such as *quesadillas* and these spicy potatoes.

8 large, very fresh oysters

1 tablespoon virgin olive oil

2 merguez sausages (or 4oz fresh chorizo) *cut into ¼-inch slices*

½ small onion *finely chopped*

1 small garlic clove *crushed*

2½ tablespoons cooked spinach

1 tablespoon HP brown sauce or spicy steak sauce

sea salt (or kosher salt) and freshly ground black pepper

1 tablespoon fresh white bread crumbs

2 tablespoons Monterey Jack cheese (or sharp cheddar) *grated*

1½ tablespoons unsalted butter *melted*

lemon wedges *for garnishing*

barbecued oysters

Barbecuing oysters is a real treat. Furthermore, with the spicy sauce quickly glazed under a rich cheese crust, this is a nice way to enjoy oysters for those who don't like them in their raw, natural state.

1 Shuck the oysters, retaining the shells, and wash thoroughly to remove any grit. Dry well.

2 Preheat the broiler to its highest setting.

3 Heat the olive oil in a nonstick frying pan. When hot, add the merguez, onion, and garlic and fry until golden in color, about 5 minutes.

4 Chop the spinach, add this to the pan, and cook for another minute. Add the spicy sauce, heat through, and season to taste.

5 Place a little of the mixture in the bottom of each oyster shell and top each with a cleaned oyster.

6 Mix together the bread crumbs, cheese, and melted butter, and spoon this over the oysters. Carefully transfer the oysters onto a baking tray and place under the preheated broiler. Cook for 3–4 minutes, until the oysters are cooked and the crust is bubbling and golden. Garnish with lemon wedges and serve.

2 tablespoons brown sugar

7oz corn flour, if unavailable use
   fine cornmeal

2 eggs

1 cup blue cheese, e.g. Roquefort or
   Gorgonzola

vegetable oil *for shallow-frying*

for the pico de gallo salsa

3 ripe, firm plum tomatoes *cut into
   small pieces*

1 clove garlic *crushed*

juice of 2 limes

1 tablespoon maple syrup

2 tablespoons freshly chopped cilantro

1 shallot *finely chopped*

sea salt (or kosher salt) and freshly
   ground black pepper

arepas with blue cheese pico de gallo

Arepas are basically a type of South American corn cake; if you can't find any corn flour, use a fine cornmeal instead. The blue cheese *pico de gallo* is my take on the classic Mexican salsa *pico de gallo*, whose essential ingredients are tomatoes, chile, and cilantro.

1 Heat 1½ cups of water in a small pan with the brown sugar and stir until dissolved. Sprinkle in the corn flour, or cornmeal, a little at a time, and beat until you have a smooth, thick dough. Beat the eggs into the dough, one at a time, then beat in half the cheese. Let it cool.

2 For the *pico de gallo*, mix all the ingredients together in a bowl and season to taste.

3 Roll lumps of the cooled dough in the palm of your hands to form small balls (2–3 inches wide). Flatten the balls gently, then fry them in hot oil in a nonstick frying pan until golden, about 4–5 minutes each side.

4 Transfer the arepas to a serving dish. Crumble over the remaining cheese and spoon the *pico de gallo* dressing on top.

4 tablespoons virgin olive oil

1 tablespoon sherry vinegar

sea salt (or kosher salt) and freshly
   ground black pepper

2 x 3¾-oz cans sardines, preserved
   in oil *drained*

2 scallions *chopped*

2 small roasted red peppers *chopped*

1 red chile *seeded and finely chopped*

½ teaspoon smoked paprika

4 slices sourdough bread

smoky sardine sandwich

Okay, so this is a toasted sandwich! But it's so simple and comforting that you'll love to make it again and again.

1 Prepare a dressing from the olive oil and vinegar, plus a little salt and pepper.

2 Place the sardines in a single layer in a dish, then scatter the onions, roasted peppers, and chile over them. Season liberally with salt, pepper, and smoked paprika, then pour the dressing on top. Cover with plastic wrap and place in the fridge for 2 hours to marinate.

3 When ready to serve, toast the bread slices, then top two of them with the sardines and vegetables. Pour a little of the marinading juices over them, then top each with the second bread slice to form a sandwich. Press down lightly to compact the filling.

4 Cut each sandwich into four wedges before serving.

coxinha

for the dough
1¼ cups chicken stock
1 cup plus 2 tablespoons flour

for the filling
2 tablespoons vegetable oil
½ small onion *finely chopped*
1 garlic clove *crushed*
7oz (about 1 cup) ground chicken
2 tablespoons cream cheese
2 tablespoons freshly chopped chives
sea salt (or kosher salt) and freshly
  ground black pepper
1 large egg white *lightly beaten*
1 cup fresh white bread crumbs
extra vegetable oil *for deep-frying*

These chicken dumplings (*coxinha* literally means "little thighs" in Portuguese) are popular all over Brazil.

1 Bring the stock to a boil, sprinkle in the flour a little at a time, then stir vigorously with a wooden spoon until amalgamated and thick and smooth in consistency.

2 Remove the dough from the pan, let it cool a little, then knead until smooth and elastic.

3 For the filling, heat the oil in a nonstick frying pan, add the onion and garlic and cook for 2 minutes until softened. Add the chicken and 2 tablespoons of water, then cook with a lid on for 5–6 minutes, until the chicken is cooked through. Transfer to a bowl and let it cool. Add the cream cheese and chives, and season to taste.

4 Roll out the dough to about 1¼ inches thick, then cut out 3-inch circles with a cookie cutter (the dough may be re-used and re-rolled).

5 To make the dumplings, take a circle of dough in the palm of your hand, fill it with the chicken mixture, then simply close up the dough.

6 Dip the dumplings in the beaten egg white, then in the bread crumbs, then deep-fry in hot oil at 300°F for 4–5 minutes, until golden. Drain on paper towels and serve.

pg tip These dumplings freeze well, but they need at least 2–3 hours to defrost completely prior to deep-frying.

8 medium-size wide-capped mushrooms *cleaned*

sea salt (or kosher salt) and freshly ground black pepper

5oz Haloumi cheese *cut into 8 slices*

for the chimichurri

2 garlic cloves *crushed*

1 tablespoooon fresh mint leaves

1 tablespoon fresh oregano leaves

a handful of flat-leaf parsley

1 small red chile *seeded and finely chopped*

3 tablespoons white wine vinegar

½ cup virgin olive oil

grilled chimichurri mushrooms with haloumi

Chimichurri is an Argentinian sauce traditionally served with grilled meats. It is similar, I suppose, to Italian pesto but without the cheese and with the addition of vinegar to give a touch of piquancy. It tastes great with mushrooms.

1 For the chimichurri sauce, put the garlic, herbs, chile, and vinegar in a small blender and mix to a coarse paste. Using the feeder tube at the top of the blender, drizzle in all but a teaspoon of the olive oil to form a thickish sauce.

2 Preheat a grill pan until hot. Brush each mushroom liberally with the chimichurri, then place on the grill pan. Cook until the mushrooms have softened and released their juices. Season to taste, then keep warm.

3 Brush the Haloumi slices with the remaining teaspoon of oil and place on the grill pan for about 2 minutes on each side, until slightly golden and crispy.

4 Place the mushrooms on a serving dish, along with the grilled cheese, and drizzle any remaining sauce over them.

1 tablespoon virgin olive oil

½ small onion *finely chopped*

½ small red chile *seeded and finely chopped*

pinch of ground cumin

9oz snapper fillet *boned, skinned, cleaned, and roughly chopped*

2 tablespoons freshly chopped cilantro

½ ripe firm mango *cut into small pieces*

2 eggs *beaten in separate bowls*

4oz Gruyère cheese (or other Swiss cheese)

12oz pie dough

snapper and mango empanadas

The empanada is really Latin America's answer to the British Cornish pasty. Be as inventive as you like and create your own fillings. This version goes well with a spicy salsa.

1 Heat the olive oil in a nonstick frying pan, add the onion, chile, and cumin, and cook gently for 2–3 minutes. Scoop into a bowl and let cool.

2 Once the onion is cool, add the chopped fish, cilantro, mango, and cheese, and bind with one of the beaten eggs. Place in the fridge for 30 minutes.

3 Preheat the oven to 350°F.

4 Roll out the dough to ⅛ inch thick, then cut out circles using a 3-inch cookie cutter. Put a spoonful of the fish mixture in the center of each circle, then brush around the edge with more beaten egg.

5 Fold the circle over to make a half-moon shape and press the edges together firmly. Brush the top with the remaining egg, place on a baking tray, and bake for 12–15 minutes, until golden. Serve warm.

12oz (about 1½ cups) very fresh crabmeat

juice of 2 limes

sea salt (or kosher salt) and freshly ground black pepper

1 tablespoon coriander seeds *lightly crushed*

2 tablespoons virgin olive oil

1 tablespoon tomato ketchup

dash of Tabasco sauce

1 small red onion *finely sliced*

2 firm ripe tomatoes *skinned, seeded and chopped*

½ cup canned corn *drained well*

6 basil leaves *chopped*

tortilla chips

¼ cup sharp cheddar cheese *grated*

crab nachos

Nachos, in their simplest form, are tortilla chips covered in melted cheese. These are an altogether much lighter version.

1 As a precaution, sift through the crabmeat to ensure that there is no hidden cartilage or shell. Place in a bowl and pour the lime juice over it. Season with salt, cover with plastic wrap, and refrigerate for 1 hour.

2 Preheat the oven to 400°F, or preheat the broiler.

3 Mix together the coriander seeds, olive oil, ketchup, Tabasco, red onion, tomatoes, and corn. Stir in the crabmeat (drained of any juices), then add the basil. Season to taste.

4 Carefully spoon the crabmeat onto the tortilla chips and place on a baking tray. Sprinkle the grated cheese over it and then bake in the oven or place under the broiler for 2–3 minutes, until the cheese is golden and bubbling.

1 tablespoon virgin olive oil

1 onion *finely chopped*

1 green chile *finely chopped*

1 teaspoon ground cumin

scant cup cooked black beans

1 recipe for Coca dough (see page 44)

1/3 cup hot salsa

2 tablespoons crème fraîche (if unavailable, use cream)

3/4 cup feta cheese *crumbled*

1/4 cup sharp cheddar cheese *grated*

picaditas

The Mexicans love their little pizzas, sold on street corners, and they are certainly addictive. Black beans are among my favorite beans, especially when cooked with onions, chile, and cumin—ingredients that epitomize for me the flavors of Mexico.

1 Preheat the oven to 400°F.

2 Heat the olive oil in a pan, then add the onion, chile, and cumin, cooking over a low heat until the onion is tender. Add the cooked beans and mix with the onions, crushing the beans lightly. Fry together for 1–2 minutes, then remove from the heat and let cool.

3 Roll out the dough to 1/4 inch thick and cut out twelve 3-inch circles using a cookie cutter. Transfer the pizza bases to a baking sheet.

4 Spread some black beans thickly onto each base, followed by some salsa. Add a spoonful of crème fraîche, then sprinkle a little of both cheeses on top. Use your fingers to crimp the edges to form a sort of pie crust.

5 Place in the oven to bake for 12–14 minutes, until the edges are lightly golden. Serve warm.

14oz purple Peruvian potatoes (also known as Peruvian blue) *washed*

1 onion *finely chopped*

5 tablespoons vegetable oil

1/2 cup flour

1 egg

sea salt (or kosher salt) and freshly ground black pepper

2/3 cup ground beef

3 scallions *finely chopped*

1 teaspoon cumin seeds

1/2 teaspoon ground cinnamon

guacamole and small leaves of watercress *for serving*

peruvian potato cakes

In Peru, these potato cakes are commonly known as *causa*. You can use normal potatoes for this recipe but the color will not be so unusual. Vegetarians could replace the meat with roasted peppers, which taste equally delicious.

1 Preheat the oven to 400°F.

2 Place the potatoes on a baking tray, bake in the oven for 40–45 minutes or until cooked through, then remove and cool slightly.

3 Fry the onion in 2 tablespoons of the oil until soft, then transfer to a bowl.

4 Peel the warm potatoes with a small knife, then add them to the onions and mash them. Add and mix in the flour, beat in the egg, and season to taste.

5 Heat the frying pan with another 2 tablespoons of oil and fry the ground beef for 6–8 minutes, until well browned all over. Add to the potatoes, along with the scallions and spices.

6 With dampened hands, shape the mixture into small patties or cakes. Heat the remaining oil in a nonstick pan and shallow-fry the potato cakes until golden and crispy, about 3–4 minutes.

7 Serve each cake topped with guacamole and a little watercress.

buljol

10oz cod fillet *boned and skinned*

2 tablespoons coarse sea salt or kosher salt

juice of 1 lime

2 shallots *finely chopped*

1 green pepper *cut in half, seeded, and cut into small pieces*

2 plum tomatoes *cut into small pieces*

4 tablespoons virgin olive oil

2 hard-boiled eggs *peeled and chopped*

1 tablespoon chopped flat-leaf parsley

1 avocado *pitted and cut into small pieces*

sea salt (or kosher salt) and freshly ground black pepper

lime wedges *for serving*

One could use the classic salt cod for this dish, as they do in the Caribbean, however I find it is better to lightly salt your own fresh cod. The result is definitely lighter, and makes a perfect salad for a hot summer's day.

1 Place the cod in a dish, scatter the sea salt over it, cover, and let it marinate at room temperature for 2 hours.

2 When the time's up, rinse the cod under a little running water to remove any excess salt, then dry well in a cloth.

3 Cut the fish into 1-inch cubes, place in a pan, and just cover with cold water. Slowly bring to a boil and simmer for 3–4 minutes. Remove the cod to a bowl using a slotted spoon and let it cool.

4 Add the remaining ingredients, toss gently together, and then let them marinate for 1 hour in the fridge for the flavors to infuse.

5 Serve the salad garnished with the lime wedges.

stuffed peppers with creole crab

2 teaspoons unsalted butter

1 small onion *finely chopped*

1 small red chile *seeded and finely chopped*

7oz crabmeat (preferably fresh) *picked over for any shells*

3 tablespoons heavy cream

pinch of curry powder

2 tablespoons fresh white bread crumbs

½ cup Gouda cheese *grated*

2oz fresh pineapple (canned is fine) *cut into small pieces*

1 tablespoon freshly chopped cilantro

8 miniature red peppers

sea salt (or kosher salt) and freshly ground black pepper

A few years ago, it would have been impossible to obtain miniature-size peppers. Now, however, they are not so hard to find. These small varieties do not always have the flavor of their more mature cousins, but they make a nice dainty boat for the crab filling.

1 Preheat the oven to 350°F.

2 Heat the butter in a pan, add the onion and chile, and cook until light and golden in color. Add the crabmeat, cream, and curry powder, and cook over a low heat until a sauce forms.

3 Stir in the bread crumbs, cheese, pineapple, and fresh cilantro, season to taste, and then set aside.

4 Cut the tops off each pepper, discard, and carefully scoop out any inner seeds. Using a teaspoon, fill each pepper with some crab mixture.

5 Stand the filled peppers in a baking pan lined with foil and cook for 12–15 minutes, or until the peppers are soft and the crab filling bubbling and golden. Let them cool slightly before serving.

peruvian salmon and tuna ceviche

9oz very fresh raw tuna fillet (sushi quality)

7oz very fresh raw salmon fillet

2 white-fleshed sweet potatoes *peeled and thinly sliced*

2 tablespoons virgin olive oil

pinch of ground cinnamon

sea salt (or kosher salt) and freshly ground black pepper

¾-inch piece ginger root *peeled and finely grated*

juice of 4 limes

1 green chile *seeded and finely chopped*

pinch of sugar

2 tablespoons freshly chopped cilantro leaves

It may sound an odd combination, but in Peru sweet potatoes are often used as an accompaniment to ceviche, especially when it is made with white fish.

1 Roll the tuna and salmon fillets separately in plastic wrap and place in the freezer for no more than 30 minutes, to firm them up a little. (This will make them easier to slice later.)

2 Preheat the oven to 400°F.

3 Place the potato slices in a bowl and toss with the olive oil, cinnamon, and salt and pepper. Transfer to a roasting pan and roast for 30 minutes, until golden and cooked through. Keep warm.

4 In a bowl, combine the ginger, lime juice, chile, sugar, and cilantro. Season to taste.

5 Take the tuna and salmon out of the freezer, and slice into ⅛-inch-thick slices using a sharp knife. Season the fish with salt and pepper, drizzle the dressing over it, then let it stand for 5 minutes. Garnish with the roasted sweet potato slices.

sardine ceviche

12 small to medium size, very fresh sardine fillets

scant cup unsweetened coconut cream

¾-inch piece ginger root *peeled and finely chopped*

juice of 3 limes

1 small red chile *seeded and finely chopped*

pinch of sugar

sea salt (or kosher salt) and freshly ground black pepper

2 firm ripe tomatoes *seeded and cut into small pieces*

2 tablespoons freshly chopped cilantro

3oz young green beans *topped and tailed*

This ceviche is inspired by the flavors of the Caribbean. Chiles, limes, and coconut make the perfect marinade for the rich, oily sardines.

1 Rinse the sardine fillets under cold running water to clean them thoroughly, then pat dry with a cloth.

2 In a bowl, whisk together the coconut cream, ginger, lime juice, chile, and sugar. Season to taste, then add the chopped tomatoes and cilantro.

3 Lay the sardines in a shallow dish, in a single layer, and pour the coconut dressing over them. Cover with plastic wrap and marinate in the fridge overnight.

4 When ready to serve, cook the green beans in boiling salted water for 4–5 minutes or until just tender; drain and refresh under cold water, then dry well.

5 Season the beans and divide between serving plates. Top with the marinated sardines and pour the dressing over them.

6 **very fresh large raw scallops** *shelled and cleaned*

½ **ripe avocado (preferably Hass variety)** *pitted*

½ **firm ripe mango** *peeled and pitted*

¼ **red pepper**

juice of 2 limes

1 **tablespoon virgin olive oil**

pinch of sugar

1 **small red chile** *seeded and finely chopped*

2 **scallions** *finely shredded*

1 **tablespoon chopped chives**

sea salt (or kosher salt) and freshly ground black pepper

scallop ceviche

Scallops are, alongside mussels, perhaps my favorite shellfish to eat and cook with, although they can be quite expensive. You must ensure complete freshness for the ceviche: do not be tempted to use the cheaper frozen ones.

1 Cut each raw scallop horizontally into five thin slices and arrange on serving plates, overlapping the slices to form a circle.

2 Cut the avocado, mango, and pepper into small pieces and place in a bowl. Add the remaining ingredients.

3 Season the scallops with sea salt and a little pepper, spoon the dressing over them, then simply let them marinate for 5 minutes before serving.

pg tip Hass avocados, which are the main variety grown in the US and New Zealand, have a dark, mottled skin and an unbeatably rich flavor: true guacamole is made from Hass avocados. For the best flavor I find that the avocados should be generally overripe when purchased.

8 medium-size, very fresh mackerel
  fillets *boned and cleaned*
1 garlic clove *crushed*
1 small green chile *chopped*
2 scallions *chopped*
a handful of fresh cilantro leaves
1 small green pepper *seeded and cut
  in pieces*
juice of 4 limes
good pinch of sugar
sea salt (or kosher salt) and freshly
  ground black pepper

for serving
1 avocado *cut in half, pitted, and
  thinly sliced*
2 tablespoons chopped chives (or
  chive shoots)

ceviche verde

For me, mackerel is one of the most underrated and under-utilized fish. It can be quite hard to find but searching it down is well worth the effort as its delicate flavor makes it the ideal vehicle for this green ceviche.

1 Slice the mackerel fillets thinly and place in a shallow serving dish.
2 In a blender, mix together the garlic, chile, scallions, and cilantro leaves until they form a paste; if necessary, use a rubber spatula to push the mixture down the sides of the blender.
3 Add the green pepper and blend again. Add the lime juice and sugar, and quickly blend one more time. Season to taste. Pour the mixture over the mackerel and let it infuse for 30 minutes.
4 Serve garnished with the sliced avocado and chives.

4 tablespoons virgin olive oil
½ teaspoon chili oil
2 tablespoons lime juice
2 scallions
¼ English cucumber *peeled and seeds
  removed*
1 red pepper *seeded*
4 shallots *peeled*
1 tablespoon Vietnamese mint *roughly
  chopped*
1 tablespoon Thai basil *roughly chopped*
12 medium-size oysters *shucked and
  cleaned on the half shell*

asian-inspired oyster ceviche

You may need to make a trip to your nearest Asian store to pick up the herbs for this dish, but I promise you won't be disappointed. It's just not the same made with regular mint and basil.

1 Combine the olive and chili oils in a bowl. Add the lime juice and mix well.
2 Finely chop the scallions and cut the red pepper and cucumber into small pieces; thinly slice the shallots.
3 Add the vegetables to the oil mixture and let them infuse for 30 minutes. Then add the herbs and the oysters and let them marinate for 5 minutes.
4 Return one oyster to each cleaned shell and spoon over it a little of the marinade. Serve immediately.

spain

No one who visits Spain could fail to fall in love with the sociable ritual of tapas, or with the exquisite dishes themselves—whether it's a simple plate of Serrano ham or a salad of octopus or sardines.

olive, anchovy, and pepper banderillas

2 large red peppers *stems removed*
12 green olives *pitted*
12 fresh anchovies marinated in oil
1 tablespoon virgin olive oil
1 teaspoon chopped fresh oregano
½ teaspoon fennel seeds
¼ teaspoon red pepper flakes
½ cup Manchego cheese *finely grated*

Banderillas, or skewers, are always a pretty addition to the table. In this recipe, the simple flavor combination brings out a real taste of Spain.

1 Preheat the oven to 425°F.
2 Cut each pepper into six, lengthwise, and place in a roasting pan. Bake in the oven for 15–20 minutes, until the peppers are cooked and their skin is blistered and blackened. Let them cool slightly, then carefully peel off the skin, taking care not to damage the flesh.
3 Wrap each olive in an anchovy fillet, then roll each inside a piece of roasted pepper. Thread each roll onto a skewer.
4 Place the skewers onto a baking tray, then drizzle the oil over them and scatter the oregano, fennel seeds, and red pepper flakes on top. Finally, sprinkle the cheese over everything and cook in the oven for 5 minutes, until the cheese is bubbling and golden.
5 Cool slightly before serving.

stuffed potatoes with snails and ham

12 small potatoes *unpeeled but well cleaned*
1½ tablespoons unsalted butter
1 shallot *finely chopped*
1 garlic clove *crushed*
5oz canned snails *drained and coarsely chopped*
2oz Serrano ham *chopped*
2 tablespoons chopped flat-leaf parsley
sea salt (or kosher salt) and freshly ground black pepper

The combination of garlicky snails with ham and potatoes may be unoriginal, but it's a marriage made in heaven.

1 Preheat the oven to 400°F.
2 Place the potatoes in a small roasting pan and bake for 30–40 minutes until cooked. Remove (leaving the oven on), and let them cool.
3 Cut the top off each potato, about ½ inch down. Using a melon baller, carefully scoop out the inner flesh of each potato, taking care not to break the outer casing.
4 In a frying pan, heat the butter until it foams, then add the shallots, garlic, and snails, and cook for 1–2 minutes. Add the ham and parsley, and season to taste.
5 Fill each potato with the mixture, and return to the oven for 5 minutes.

for the dough

1⅓ cups strong white bread flour

½ cup fine cornmeal

sea salt (or kosher salt)

½ teaspoon sugar

1 x ¼-oz envelope rapid-rise yeast

2 teaspoons virgin olive oil

1 red onion *peeled and finely chopped*

3oz pumpkin *skinned and thinly sliced*

1 tablespoon red wine vinegar

2 tablespoons tomato paste

2 roasted red peppers *drained (oil reserved) and cut into ¼-inch squares*

1 teaspoon smoked paprika

2 tablespoons grated manchego cheese

coca

Coca is the name of a type of Spanish pizza, traditionally baked in a wooden oven and topped with all sorts of delicious things. The smoked paprika gives a wonderful woodsmoke flavor and an authentic Spanish note.

1 Sift the flour into a bowl and add two thirds of the cornmeal, a pinch of salt, and the sugar and yeast. Make a well in the center, pour in ⅔ cup warm water, and bring the ingredients together to form a soft, pliable dough.

2 Turn the dough out onto a floured surface and knead gently for 5–6 minutes. Return the dough to the bowl, cover it with plastic wrap, then let it rise in a warm place for 1 hour.

3 Preheat the oven to 400°F.

4 Sprinkle a large baking sheet with the remaining cornmeal. Roll out the dough to roughly 8 x 12 inches, and transfer it to the baking sheet.

5 Heat the olive oil in a pan, add the onion, and cook for 5 minutes, until softened. Add the pumpkin slices, cooking gently for another 5 minutes, until lightly caramelized. Stir in the red wine vinegar and simmer for 2 minutes.

6 Spread the tomato paste over the dough and top with the onion and pumpkin mixture, followed by the roasted peppers. Sprinkle the smoked paprika over it.

7 Drizzle the reserved pepper oil over everything and place the *cocas* in the oven to bake for 12–15 minutes, until golden. Scatter the Manchego cheese on top and bake for another 5 minutes.

10oz fresh chorizo sausages

1 cup flour

1 teaspoon rapid-rise yeast

1 egg *beaten*

sea salt (or kosher salt)

vegetable oil *for deep-frying*

½ cup aïoli (see page 59) *for serving*

buñuelos

These fritters originated in Spain, but you also find them in Mexico and other parts of Latin America. They are made with a wheat-based dough and are traditionally sweet, but there are savory versions too—some made with cheese or, as here, spicy chorizo.

1 Cut the sausages into ¾-inch-thick slices.

2 Make a batter with the flour, yeast, egg, and ⅓ cup water. Season with a little salt.

3 Heat the oil to 325°F.

4 Dip the sausage chunks in the batter, then immerse them in the hot oil. Fry until they are golden and crispy, then drain on paper towels. Serve with the aïoli.

jabugo ham with pineapple and valdeon cheese

4 thick slices country bread
2 tablespoons virgin olive oil
4oz fresh pineapple *skin removed*
1 teaspoon brown sugar
4oz Valdeon cheese *thinly sliced*
8 slices Jabugo ham

Jabugo ham tastes sensational and is undoubtedly Spain's greatest ham. It is expensive, however, so you could use Serrano or prosciutto instead for this recipe. Valdeon (also known as Picos de Europa) is a Spanish blue cheese, similar to Roquefort in taste and appearance.

1 Heat a grill pan until very hot. Brush the bread slices with the olive oil and place on the grill to toast on both sides until charred.

2 Cut the pineapple into semi-circles, sprinkle liberally with brown sugar, then place on the grill pan until lightly caramelized. Remove from the heat and cut into small chunks.

3 Top the toasts with the cheese, lay the sliced ham on top, then garnish with the grilled pineapple.

tuna and goat cheese empanadillas

1 teaspoon virgin olive oil
1 small onion *finely chopped*
1 garlic clove *crushed*
5oz cooked new potatoes *peeled*
1 x 6¼-oz can tuna in oil *drained*
3oz soft goat cheese
6 green olives *pitted and chopped*
2 teaspoons superfine capers *rinsed and drained*
a little paprika
sea salt (or kosher salt) and freshly ground black pepper
12oz pie dough
a little beaten egg

Empanadillas are smaller, pocket-size versions of *empanadas*, and are the ideal party food. Understandably perhaps, they are often associated with South America, but in fact they originated in Spain's northern region of Galicia, where they are still popular.

1 Preheat the oven to 400°F.

2 Heat the olive oil in a frying pan over a low heat. Add the onion and garlic and cook for 4–5 minutes, until softened, then remove to a large bowl. Let it cool.

3 Add the potatoes and lightly crush with a fork. Add the tuna, goat cheese, olives, and capers, mixing gently together. Add the paprika and season to taste.

4 Roll out the dough on a floured surface to ⅛-inch thick, then cut out 20–25 circles using a 3-inch cookie cutter.

5 Place a good spoonful of the mixture in the middle of each pastry dough circle, brush the edges with egg, then bring up the sides to meet at the top to form a small package, turnover style. Crimp the empanadilla along the top to secure the filling.

6 Brush with some beaten egg and bake on a baking tray for 12–15 minutes, until golden and flaky.

pg tip If you don't want to cook the empanadillas right away, the uncooked empanadillas can be kept in the fridge for 1–2 days, or for up to one month in the freezer.

squid meatballs with saffron

10oz (about 1¼ cups) squid tubes
 cleaned and roughly chopped
1 small onion *finely chopped*
2 tablespoons chopped flat-leaf parsley
2 tablespoons dry sherry
sea salt (or kosher salt) and freshly
 ground black pepper
7oz lean ground pork
3oz dry and fine white bread crumbs
1 egg *beaten*
2 tablespoons virgin olive oil

for the sauce
3 tablespoons virgin olive oil
1 garlic clove *crushed*
good pinch of saffron threads
2 tablespoons flour
¾ cup fish stock

The recipe for these tasty meatballs, which hails from Andalucía, was given to me by a Spanish chef friend of mine. I always found the combination of squid and pork somewhat daunting, but they both have the same glutinous texture and so complement each other well. In Spain, pork is often combined with seafood such as squid, clams, mussels, and shrimp.

1 Place the chopped squid in a food processor and blend to a coarse paste. Transfer to a bowl and add the onion, parsley, sherry, and seasoning. Refrigerate for 30 minutes.
2 For the sauce, heat the oil with the garlic and saffron for about 1 minute. Stir in the flour and cook for 20 seconds before adding the fish stock. Mix well to form a sauce, simmer for 15 minutes, then strain.
3 Mix the squid with the ground pork, bread crumbs, and egg, and shape into 1-inch balls.
4 Heat the olive oil in a frying pan. When hot, gently fry the squid balls until golden, about 5–6 minutes.
5 Serve the squid and pork balls with the saffron sauce spooned over them—they look lovely presented on small spoons.

2 tablespoons virgin olive oil

1 garlic clove *crushed*

pinch of paprika

sea salt (or kosher salt) and freshly ground black pepper

16 large raw jumbo shrimp *shelled and deveined (tails kept on, heads removed)*

for the mojo verde

1 garlic clove *crushed*

a small handful of cilantro *leaves only*

a small handful of flat-leaf parsley

1 small green pepper *seeded and cut into small pieces*

⅓ cup virgin olive oil

2 tablespoons red wine vinegar

shrimp a la plancha with mojo verde

Cooking *a la plancha* simply means cooking on a hot grill—a quick and easy way to seal in flavor. The *mojo verde* (green sauce) comes from the Canary Islands, where it is normally served with fish.

1 Mix the olive oil, garlic, paprika, and salt and pepper in a dish. Add the shrimp, toss well, and leave it for 30 minutes to marinate.

2 For the mojo verde, place the garlic, cilantro, and parsley in a blender and puree. Add the pepper, olive oil, and vinegar, and blend again until smooth. Season to taste.

3 Heat a grill pan and, when very hot, add the shrimp and cook for 2–3 minutes, turning occasionally. Serve them hot from the grill with the green sauce.

2 tablespoons virgin olive oil
½ onion *finely chopped*
1 garlic clove *crushed*
1 small green pepper *seeded and cut into ½-inch cubes*
1 small red pepper *seeded and cut into ½-inch cubes*
2 firm ripe tomatoes *cut into ½-inch cubes*
4 eggs *lightly beaten*
sea salt (or kosher salt) and freshly ground black pepper
2 slices country bread *cut into ½-inch cubes*
3oz Serrano ham *chopped*
1 tablespoon chopped flat-leaf parsley

piperrada

Egg dishes provide a cheap and nutritious meal and are popular throughout Spain. This omelette-cum-pepper stew recipe comes from the Basque region, and is great for breakfast or brunch.

1 Heat half the olive oil in a frying pan. Add the onion, garlic, and peppers, and cook for 5–6 minutes, or until the peppers have softened and taken on a little color. Add the tomatoes and cook for another 2 minutes.
2 Raise the heat, then pour in the beaten eggs, allowing them to set a little before gently folding them in with the vegetables. Season to taste.
3 Heat the remaining oil in another frying pan and add the bread cubes, ham, and parsley. Cook until the bread is lightly golden.
4 Spoon the eggs onto serving dishes and top with the bread mixture.

2 eggs *hard-boiled and peeled*
2 ripe firm tomatoes *chopped*
1 small onion *chopped*
1 small green pepper *seeded and cut into ½-inch dice*
1 small red pepper *seeded and cut into ½-inch dice*
1 garlic clove *crushed*
1 tablespoon white wine vinegar
4 tablespoons olive oil
2 tablespoons chopped flat-leaf parsley
1 tablespoon chopped basil
9oz pack cooked seafood selection
sea salt (or kosher salt) and freshly ground black pepper

gazpacho seafood salad

This salad is fresh and extremely appetizing. It uses some of Spain's most typical cooking ingredients to great effect.

1 Cut the eggs in half, remove the cooked yolk, mash it with a fork, and place it to one side; chop the cooked white.
2 Place the tomatoes, onion, peppers, and chopped egg whites in a bowl.
3 Mix the garlic, cooked egg yolk, vinegar, and oil to form a dressing. Add the herbs and then stir into the tomato mixture.
4 Finally, throw in the cooked seafood and season to taste.

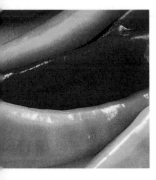

px glazed pork

1 small pork fillet (or sliced pork belly) *cut into ¾-inch cubes*
1 clove garlic *crushed*
1 teaspoon freshly picked oregano
1 tablespoon olive oil
2 tablespoons vegetable oil
12oz (about 3 cups) baby onions
sea salt (or kosher salt) and freshly ground black pepper
4 slices of bacon *roughly chopped*
½ cup Pedro Ximénez (or other sweet) sherry

I adore Pedro Ximénez sherry in dishes. It is wonderfully sweet and rich, and works really well with pork. The recipe could be made with chicken if you prefer.

1 Marinate the pork in a bowl with the garlic, oregano, and olive oil for 1 hour.
2 Heat the vegetable oil in a large nonstick frying pan. When hot, add the onions and fry for 4–5 minutes, until golden. Set aside.
3 Return the pan to the heat, season the pork with salt and pepper, and fry in the pan for 4–5 minutes. Add the bacon and cook for another 2 minutes.
4 Return the onions to the pan, pour the sherry over them, and cook with the lid on for 4–5 minutes, until the meat and onions are cooked and the sauce has reduced to a glaze. Transfer to a serving dish and pour the pan juices over the meat and onions.

calamari with chorizo and salsa verde

18oz small squid *cleaned*
2 tablespoons virgin olive oil
4oz fresh chorizo *thinly sliced*
²⁄₃ cup cooked white beans (canned is fine)

for the salsa verde
2 garlic cloves *crushed*
2oz flat-leaf parsley
2oz fresh basil leaves
1 anchovy fillet
1 tablespoon superfine capers
1 tablespoon white wine vinegar
4 tablespoons extra virgin olive oil
1 hard-boiled egg *roughly chopped*
sea salt (or kosher salt) and freshly ground black pepper

Capers and anchovies are the signature ingredients of *salsa verde*, which packs much more of a punch than the *mojo verde* on page 51. It is one of the tastiest of sauces, and goes wonderfully with the calamari, while the chorizo adds a little spice to the dish.

1 To prepare the squid, cut off the fins, then pull the bag and the tentacles apart. Remove the backbone and any soft innards from the bag. Cut away the head from the tentacles, and discard. Rinse the squid in cold water and dry in a cloth. Slice thinly and set aside.
2 For the green sauce, place the garlic, herbs, and anchovy in a small blender and blend to a coarse pulp. Add the capers and blend quickly again. Transfer to a bowl and add the vinegar and oil to form a semi-liquid sauce. Finally, add the egg and season to taste.
3 Heat the olive oil in a large nonstick pan over a high heat, add the chorizo and fry until slightly crispy. Add the squid and cook for another 2 minutes, still on a high heat.
4 Quickly add the cooked beans and green sauce and toss together. Transfer to a dish and serve immediately.

pg tip Chorizo comes either cooked (and ready-to-eat) or uncooked. The latter, which is the only type used in this book, is normally sold as a string of small sausages, which you can slice up and add to all sorts of savory dishes.

1¼lb large plump mussels *cleaned and debearded*

1 bottle Spanish beer (or another light beer)

6 slices of bacon

2 eggs *beaten*

4oz (1¼ cups) dry and fine white bread crumbs

1 tablespoon virgin olive oil

3½ tablespoons unsalted butter

2 tablespoons chopped flat-leaf parsley

sea salt (or kosher salt) and freshly ground black pepper

mussels with bacon and cerveza

When preparing this dish, try to find the largest, plumpest mussels available: wrapping up a tiny mussel in bacon would be a very fiddly job!

1 Place the mussels in a hot pan over a high heat. Pour the beer over them, cover quickly with a lid, and cook until the mussels open, about 2–3 minutes. Remove from the heat and strain, reserving the cooking liquor. Let the mussels cool.

2 Remove the cold mussels from their shells. Cut the bacon slices in half and wrap each half around one mussel.

3 Dip the wrapped mussels in the beaten egg, then in the bread crumbs. Thread them equally onto four presoaked bamboo skewers.

4 Heat the olive oil with half the butter in a frying pan, lay the skewers in the pan, and cook for 2–3 minutes on each side, until golden. Transfer to a serving plate.

5 Add the reserved mussel juices and the remaining butter to the pan, and boil together for 1 minute. Sprinkle in the chopped parsley and then pour the sauce around the skewered mussels when ready to serve.

pg tip Remember to discard any mussels that are open when purchased, as these are dead, and again discard any that remain closed once they have been cooked.

4oz sweet Ogen (green-fleshed) melon *peeled, seeded and cut into ½-inch cubes*

4oz sweet Cantaloupe or Charentais (orange-fleshed) melon *peeled, seeded and cut into ½-inch cubes*

2oz watermelon *peeled, seeded and cut into ½-inch cubes*

1 tablespoon virgin olive oil

10oz good-quality fresh chorizo *thickly sliced*

½ cup dry sherry

sea salt (or kosher salt) and freshly ground black pepper

2 tablespoons freshly chopped mint

chorizo with sweet melon and mint

I just love the way the spicy and sweet pair together in this dish. It's a real winner.

1 Heat the olive oil in a large frying pan and fry the chorizo slices until they are brown and crisp on the outside but still juicy within. (The chorizo yields plenty of its own fat, so don't overdo the olive oil.)

2 Add the melon pieces, quickly toss together, then pour in the sherry. Let it bubble up for 30 seconds. Add 2 tablespoons of water and cook for another minute. Season with a touch of salt and black pepper.

3 Transfer to a serving dish and sprinkle the mint over it.

3 tablespoons virgin olive oil

juice of ½ lemon

1 tablespoon white wine vinegar

2 small garlic cloves *thinly sliced*

sea salt (or kosher salt) and freshly ground black pepper

10oz fresh anchovies *cleaned*

4 eggs

1 tablespoon freshly chopped flat-leaf parsley

for the aïoli

⅔ cup good-quality mayonnaise

2 garlic cloves *crushed*

boquerones with soft-boiled eggs and aïoli

Boquerones are small fresh anchovies from Spain. They are delicious marinated, particularly when smothered with the yolk oozing out of soft-boiled eggs.

1 Prepare the marinade by mixing the oil, lemon juice, vinegar, garlic, and salt and pepper.

2 Fillet the anchovies with a small knife, then lay the fillets in a dish. Pour the marinade over them, cover, and leave for 4 hours.

3 Make the aïoli by mixing the mayonnaise and garlic together in a bowl.

4 When ready to serve, soft boil the eggs in a large pan of simmering water, for 3–4 minutes. Remove with a slotted spoon and run under cold water for 30 seconds to cool the eggs enough for you to peel them.

5 Arrange the eggs in a serving dish, garnished with the marinated anchovies. Sprinkle the parsley over them and serve with the garlic mayonnaise alongside.

pg tip The best way to fillet a fresh anchovy is to simply pull the head of each anchovy firmly down through the belly and towards the tail. This releases the spine, leaving the fish split in a butterfly fashion.

10oz fresh squid *cleaned and tentacles removed*

2 tablespoons virgin olive oil

1 onion *finely chopped*

2 garlic cloves *crushed*

1 teaspoon smoked paprika

¾ cup paella or risotto rice

3¼ cups fish stock

3 sachets squid ink (ask at your local fish market)

1 lemon *cut into wedges for serving*

for the saffron allioli

pinch of saffron threads *soaked in boiling water*

1 garlic clove *crushed*

⅓ cup good-quality mayonnaise

black paella

Don't be put off by the sound of the squid ink used in this recipe (it adds a little saltiness and works with the rice to great effect), nor by the fish stock: excellent fresh stocks are available in gourmet supermarkets and specialty food stores these days. The *allioli* is simply a Catalan version of aïoli (garlic mayonnaise).

1 Cut the squid into rings. Heat half the olive oil in a heavy pan until very hot. Add the squid and cook for 1 minute until sealed all over. (If you cook the squid for any longer it will turn rubbery.) Set aside.

2 Add the onion and garlic to the pan, along with the remaining olive oil and the paprika, and cook gently for 1–2 minutes. Add the rice and stir until it is well coated with the oil, onion, and paprika.

3 Heat up the fish stock in a pan, add the squid ink, then pour this over the rice. Lower the heat to barely a simmer and cook for 15–18 minutes, until nearly all the liquid has been absorbed and the rice is al dente. Return the squid to the rice and mix well.

4 For the allioli, mix the saffron and garlic into the mayonnaise, stir well, and serve with the paella, along with lemon wedges.

---

2 little romaine lettuces *leaves separated, washed, dried, and torn into small pieces*

2 stalks of celery *thinly sliced*

4 scallions *shredded*

4oz good-quality cooked ham *cut into strips*

2 roasted red peppers in oil *drained and chopped*

2 slices country bread *toasted and cut into small cubes*

½ cup Manchego cheese *finely grated*

for the dressing

5 marinated fresh anchovies

⅓ cup mayonnaise

1 garlic clove *crushed*

1 tablespoon red wine vinegar

dash of Worcestershire sauce

sea salt (or kosher salt) and freshly ground black pepper

spanish caesar salad

A simple play on the classic Caesar salad, loved the world over.

1 In a bowl, mix the ingredients for the dressing together, and season to taste.

2 In another bowl, toss together the lettuce, celery, scallions, ham, peppers, and toasted bread. Pour the dressing over them and toss well.

3 Arrange the salad on serving plates and sprinkle the Manchego cheese over them.

1/3 cup virgin olive oil

2 shallots *thinly sliced*

good pinch of saffron threads
   (or ½ teaspoon powdered variety)

10oz chestnut or button mushrooms
   cut in half (or, if large, quartered)

2 tablespoons white wine vinegar
   (or rice wine vinegar)

1 tablespoon sugar

1 teaspoon crushed coriander seeds

½ teaspoon black peppercorns *lightly cracked*

1 small bay leaf

1 small jar artichoke halves in oil
   drained (reserving the oil)

1 tablespoon flat-leaf parsley leaves

mushroom and artichoke escabeche

Escabeche is a Spanish term for food (usually fish or vegetables) that is lightly soused or pickled. This dish is ideal for vegetarians.

1 Heat the oil in a frying pan over a low heat, add the shallots and saffron, and fry for 4–5 minutes, until the shallots begin to caramelize to a light golden brown.

2 Add the mushrooms and cook for another 5–6 minutes, or until the mushrooms are brown and just cooked through.

3 Add the vinegar, sugar, coriander seeds, peppercorns, bay leaf, and 1/3 cup water. Cover with a lid and simmer for 8 minutes.

4 Remove the lid, add the artichoke halves plus a little of the oil from the jar, cover again, and cook for 5 minutes more.

5 Remove from the heat, transfer to a dish, and let cool to room temperature. Scatter the parsley leaves over it before serving.

1 green pepper *seeded and cut into thick strips*

1 red pepper *seeded and cut into thick strips*

1 small eggplant *cut into ½-inch cubes*

2 garlic cloves *crushed*

1 teaspoon fresh oregano *chopped*

1/3 cup olive oil

2 tablespoons sherry vinegar

pinch of sugar

4 slices sourdough bread

1 large very ripe and juicy tomato

sea salt (or kosher salt)

Manchego cheese shavings *for serving*

spanish-style bruschetta

A Spanish version of the classic Italian bruschetta—a contradiction in terms, perhaps, but delicious all the same. Vegetables work beautifully in this recipe, and fish such as sardines and anchovies would go well, too.

1 Preheat the oven to 400°F.

2 Place the peppers, eggplant cubes, and half the crushed garlic in a roasting pan. Scatter the oregano over them and drizzle half the oil on top, then place in the oven for 25–30 minutes, until the vegetables are charred and cooked through.

3 Transfer the vegetables to a bowl and add the vinegar and sugar. Let them marinate for 2 hours.

4 To serve, heat the remaining olive oil in a large nonstick frying pan and fry the slices of bread until golden and crisp. Remove from the pan and smear the remaining crushed garlic on the bread.

5 Next, squeeze and crush the tomato over the surface of the bread, and sprinkle with sea salt.

6 Arrange the vegetables neatly on the tomato toasts, drizzle any juices over them, and place the cheese shavings on top.

1 tablespoon virgin olive oil
1 shallot *finely chopped*
16–20 fresh razor clams
sea salt (or kosher salt) and freshly
  ground black pepper

for the romesco
2 dried red peppers *seeded and soaked
  in water for 1 hour*
1/3 cup virgin olive oil
1 red chile *chopped*
3 garlic cloves *crushed*
1 slice white bread *cut into 1-inch
  pieces*
3 tablespoons blanched almonds *toasted*
1 tablespoon tomato paste
2 tablespoons white wine vinegar
sea salt (or kosher salt)

razor clams with romesco sauce

Razor clams are not always readily available, but an Asian supermarket or specialty gourmet store should stock them. It's worth seeking them out, they are delicious! Eat them grilled just with lemon and olive oil, or as they are here, topped with one of Spain's greatest sauces, *romesco*.

1 For the romesco, first drain and dry the peppers, then chop finely. Heat half the olive oil in a frying pan and fry the peppers and fresh chile, taking care not to burn them. Set aside. In the same oil, fry the garlic and bread until golden, then set aside.

2 Place the almonds and tomato paste in a blender, along with the pepper and bread mixtures, and mix to a smooth paste. Add the remaining oil and vinegar, and season with salt.

3 When ready to serve, heat the olive oil in a frying pan, add the shallot, cook for 1–2 minutes, then add the clams. Pour in 1/3 cup water, cover with a lid, and cook until the shells open, about 2 minutes.

4 Transfer the clams to a serving dish, add the romesco sauce to the cooking juices in the pan and adjust the seasoning. Pour the sauce over the clams when ready to serve.

pg tip Dried peppers—traditionally mild nora chile peppers from Spain—are the most important ingredient in romesco sauce. You can find them in good delis, but if you need to substitute, you could use ¼ teaspoon of red pepper flakes.

⅓ cup flour

¼ teaspoon baking powder

3 scallions *finely chopped*

2 tablespoons chopped flat-leaf parsley

9oz peeled brown small shrimp or regular shrimp

sea salt (or kosher salt) and freshly ground black pepper

a little paprika

vegetable oil *for frying*

crispy shrimp pancakes

This is an unusual dish of tiny brown shrimp crisply fried in a light onion and parsley batter, which I first tasted in a tapas bar in Alicante, southern Spain. The generous sprinkling of sea salt before serving is essential.

1 Place the flour and baking powder in a bowl, add ⅓ cup water and stir to a smooth batter.

2 Add the scallions, parsley, and shrimp, and season with salt, pepper, and paprika. Let stand, covered, for 1 hour in the fridge.

3 Pour enough vegetable oil in the bottom of a frying pan to reach a depth of ½ inch, and place over a high heat. When the oil is hot, add spoonfuls of batter and fry until golden, turning the pancakes over with a spatula to cook both sides.

4 Drain the pancakes on paper towels and sprinkle liberally with sea salt.

14oz (about 3 cups) new potatoes *unpeeled*

1 onion *finely chopped*

2 garlic cloves *crushed*

2 tablespoons sherry vinegar

⅔ cup virgin olive oil

1 x 6¼-oz can of tuna in oil *drained*

2 tablespoons chopped flat-leaf parsley

sea salt (or kosher salt) and freshly ground black pepper

garlic bread *for serving*

tuna and potato salad

I rarely open a can of anything as a rule, but for this salad "dip" preserved tuna works best. Just make sure you buy the best quality tuna you can find.

1 Place the potatoes in a pan of boiling salted water and cook for 15–20 minutes. Drain in a colander and let the potatoes cool enough for you to peel them comfortably.

2 Place the potatoes in a food processor, add the onion, garlic, vinegar, half the oil and half the tuna, and blitz to a paste.

3 With the motor running, drizzle in the remaining oil through the feeder tube at the top of the processor, to form a smooth puree.

4 Transfer to a serving dish, scatter the remaining tuna over it, sprinkle the parsley on top, and season. Serve at room temperature with slices of crisp garlic bread.

14oz (about 3 cups) waxy potatoes, *peeled*

5 tablespoons virgin olive oil

1 onion *very thinly sliced*

2 garlic cloves *crushed*

6 large eggs

sea salt (or kosher salt) and freshly ground black pepper

mini potato tortillas

Although a common dish, tortilla is easy to make badly. The key to this recipe is making sure that you let the potatoes soak properly in the egg mixture (softening them in the process). You could, of course, use a small frying pan if you don't have any small tart pans.

1 Slice the potatoes very thinly using a mandoline slicer or a sharp knife. Dry them on paper towels.

2 Heat the olive oil in a large nonstick frying pan over medium heat. Throw in the potato slices, onion, and garlic, and cook for 15–20 minutes, or until the potatoes are tender and the onions lightly caramelized.

3 Beat the eggs in a bowl with a generous sprinkle of salt and pepper. Gently stir the potatoes into the eggs and set aside for 10–15 minutes.

4 Preheat the oven to 350°F.

5 Lightly oil eight 2¾-inch tart pans all over (Yorkshire pudding or muffin pans will do if necessary), then fill with the egg and potato mixture.

6 Place on a baking sheet and bake for 12–15 minutes, or until just set. Loosen the tortillas, then remove, or alternatively eat them from the pans.

pg tip You can add some chorizo to the onion to give these tortillas an extra touch of heat. They are great eaten hot or cold, and taste good with garlic mayonnaise.

2¼ cups cava (or sparkling wine)

¼ small cucumber *cut in half lengthwise then thinly sliced*

pinch of sea salt (or kosher salt)

12 oysters *shucked and cleaned*

⅓oz caviar (optional luxury)

chilled oysters with cava granita

Here's a sexy dish if ever there was one: cool, briny oysters, cucumber, and caviar, all offset with iced cava shavings. This dish is one big treat for the taste buds!

1 Mix 1¼ cups water with the cava in a small shallow container and place in the freezer. Put the cucumber and salt into a bowl to extract excess water.

2 After 30 minutes, remove the emerging cava granita from the freezer and mix it around with a fork to break up the granules. Return it to the freezer for 2 hours, stirring occasionally.

3 Remove the oysters from their shells. Wash and dry the shells, reserving enough for each oyster to be served on the half shell.

4 Place a bed of cucumber in each half shell, then top with an oyster.

5 Break up the granita again, then spoon some onto each oyster. Top with the caviar, if using. Eat in one mouthful for the ultimate experience.

3oz sunblush or sundried tomatoes in oil *drained*

1 head of fennel *peeled and cut into ½-inch wedges*

1 garlic clove *sliced*

1 small bay leaf

2 tablespoons virgin olive oil

sea salt (or kosher salt) and freshly ground black pepper

⅓ cup water

3½ tablespoons white wine vinegar

⅓ cup dry white wine

7oz baby clams

12oz mussels

6oz baby squid *tentacles removed and cleaned*

seafood escabeche

The word *escabeche* is thought to have originated in Persia, where it was used to describe a dish of poached or fried fish served with its acidic marinade. You'll find a similar dish elsewhere, too, including the *escovitch* of Jamaica and the *scapece* of Italy.

1 Preheat the oven to 350°F.

2 Place the vegetables, garlic, and bay leaf in a roasting pan or casserole dish. Pour in half the olive oil and toss well. Season with salt and pepper, then place in the oven to cook for 30 minutes, until lightly caramelized.

3 In a large pot, bring the water, wine vinegar, and white wine, plus a little sea salt, to a boil. Add the seafood, drizzle the remaining oil over it, and cook with a lid on for 1–2 minutes, until the seafood is cooked. Remove from the heat and let cool.

4 Arrange the vegetables in a shallow dish, followed by the seafood. Spoon over some of the poaching liquid and top with freshly ground black pepper.

europe

Small plates in Europe range from the antipasti of Italy to the *amuses-bouche* of France and the *smorgasbord* of Sweden. They share a respect for fresh ingredients and an emphasis on harmonious flavor combinations.

russian omelette

2 teaspoons unsalted butter

2 small onions *thinly sliced*

9oz (about 2 cups) new potatoes *boiled, peeled, and thickly sliced*

¼ teaspoon dill seeds

8 eggs

½ cup heavy cream

sea salt (or kosher salt) and freshly ground black pepper

8oz smoked salmon (lox) *finely chopped*

sour cream

fresh dill *for garnishing*

a little caviar (optional)

Why Russian you say? I wanted to include an egg-based dish with smoked salmon... smoked salmon led me to caviar (why not?) ... and that led to sour cream... and then the dish suddenly became obvious.

1 Melt the butter in a 10-inch nonstick frying pan or omelette pan, add the onions and cook over a low heat until golden, about 5–6 minutes. Add the cooked potatoes and dill seeds.

2 Preheat the broiler to a medium heat.

3 Beat the eggs in a bowl, add the heavy cream, and season to taste with salt and pepper. Pour half the eggs into the pan and scatter the smoked salmon on top. Cook for a few minutes or until the omelette begins to set, then pour in the remaining eggs and cook for another 5–6 minutes.

4 Remove from the heat and place under the preheated broiler until the omelette rises and browns.

5 Transfer the omelette to a board and cut into wedges. Serve with sour cream and a scattering of fresh dill. For a taste of real luxury, you could add a spoonful of caviar in between.

star anise-cured salmon

8 star anise pods

3 tablespoons sugar

3 tablespoons sea salt (or kosher salt)

18oz very fresh thick salmon fillets *skinless*

2 lemons *very thinly sliced*

for the dipping sauce

⅔ cup good-quality mayonnaise

1 cooked beet *chopped*

½ teaspoon Dijon mustard

1 teaspoon honey

I first came across the pairing of star anise with salmon in Stockholm. Here, it is ground up and added to salt and sugar to form the cure for a gravlax-style marinade.

Note: This recipe requires overnight marinating.

1 Place the star anise pods in a mortar, or in a small coffee grinder, and crush to a fine powder. Add the sugar and salt, then rub the mixture over the salmon fillets.

2 Top the salmon with the lemon slices, then wrap tightly in foil. Place on a tray in the fridge to marinate overnight.

3 For the dipping sauce, place all the ingredients in a blender and puree to a smooth sauce. Season to taste.

4 Take the salmon out of the fridge, remove the lemon slices, and scrape off any remaining spice mixture. Slice the fillet into ¼-inch-thick slices, arrange on a dish and serve with the dipping sauce.

pg tip For an alternative presentation for this recipe, you could cut the cured salmon into cubes and thread it onto wooden skewers.

½ cup (1 stick) unsalted butter

1 cup plus 2 tablespoons flour *sifted*

4 eggs *beaten*

5oz Stilton cheese

3oz Gruyère cheese (or other Swiss cheese)

sea salt (or kosher salt) and freshly ground black pepper

vegetable oil *for deep-frying*

stilton fritters

Stilton cheese is one of Britain's greatest treasures. These little fritters are a great way to use up any trimmings or small pieces left from a cheese board.

1 Bring 1¼ cups water to the boil. Add the butter, then quickly sprinkle in the flour and beat with a wooden spoon until the mixture leaves the side of the pan. Remove from the heat.

2 Beat the eggs into the mixture in three stages, beating well each time. Then, while the mixture is still warm, beat in the cheeses. Season well.

3 Heat the oil in a pan to 325°F. Fry the fritters in batches, dropping spoonfuls of the batter into the hot oil and cooking until golden.

4 Drain on paper towels, then serve.

pg tip These Stilton fritters taste delicious with plum chutney, or even apple or a good tomato chutney. Vegetable or beet pickles would make a good accompaniment, too.

---

1 large eggplant

1 garlic clove *peeled and thinly sliced*

6 tablespoons virgin olive oil

1 small onion *finely chopped*

1 small red pepper *chopped*

½ small green pepper *chopped*

2 ripe firm tomatoes *seeded and chopped*

½ teaspoon sugar

juice of ¼ lemon

sea salt (or kosher salt) and freshly black ground pepper

ikra

This Russian eggplant salad is equally good served as a spread; simply blend it at the final stage. In Russia, the traditional accompaniment is dark rye or pumpernickel bread.

1 Preheat the oven to 425°F.

2 Using a small knife, pierce holes randomly into the eggplant and fill the holes with the thinly sliced garlic.

3 Rub some olive oil over the eggplant and place on a baking tray. Bake in the oven for 1 hour, turning occasionally, until the eggplant is charred and blistered.

4 Meanwhile, heat 3 tablespoons of the oil in a pan, add the onion, and cook for 5–6 minutes until softened. Add the peppers, cook for another 5 minutes until softened, then transfer to a bowl.

5 Remove the skin carefully from the eggplant, then chop the pulp finely until almost a puree. Add this to the pepper mixture.

6 Stir in the tomatoes, sugar, lemon juice, and remaining olive oil. Season with salt and pepper.

1 tablespoon vegetable oil

1 small onion *finely chopped*

½ teaspoon freshly picked thyme

2 slices of back bacon *chopped*

2 tablespoons raisins *soaked in water until plump, drained*

1 Granny Smith apple *peeled, cored, and chopped*

6oz black pudding (blood sausage)

sea salt (or kosher salt) and freshly ground black pepper

10oz pie dough

a little beaten egg

black pudding, apple, and bacon pies

Whenever I serve these little pies alongside drinks, they seem to disappear in no time. I suggest you prepare them in bulk, as you're bound to eat more than you think, and they also freeze well.

1 Heat the oil in a frying pan. When hot, add the onion and thyme and cook for 5–6 minutes, until the onions are softened.

2 Raise the heat, add the bacon, raisins, and apple, and fry until the bacon is cooked and the apple caramelized. Finally, add the black pudding. Mix well together and cook until the mixture is well mashed up. Season to taste, remove from the heat, and let cool.

3 Preheat the oven to 400°F. Lightly oil 12–15 small tartlet molds (a mini muffin pan is also fine).

4 Roll out the dough to ¹/₈-inch thick, then cut out twelve circles using a 2½-inch cookie cutter. Cut out another twelve circles, using a 2-inch cookie cutter, for the tops.

5 Line the molds with the larger dough circles, then add a spoonful of the black pudding mixture. Brush around the edges of the dough with the beaten egg before toppping each pie with a smaller circle of dough. Press down gently to seal and brush with the remaining egg.

6 Using a small knife, make a couple of slits in the top of each pie, then bake for 12–15 minutes, until golden. Let stand for a moment or two before removing from the mold and serving.

12 quails' eggs

2 tablespoons coarse sea salt (or kosher salt)

1 tablespoon freshly chopped chives

¼ teaspoon smoked paprika

quails' eggs with smoked and spiced sea salt

Quails' eggs have suddenly become trendy, and are now widely available here. They have a delicate, almost gamey flavor and taste wonderful either soft or hard-boiled.

1 Bring a pan of water to a boil, carefully immerse the quails' eggs, and reduce the heat to a simmer. Cook the eggs for 4 minutes, then remove and immediately refresh in iced water.

2 Carefully peel the eggs and place on individual spoons or, alternatively, pile them in a bowl.

3 Mix the sea salt, chives, and paprika, sprinkle a little on each egg and serve.

pg tip Other ways to serve quails' eggs include: with celery salt, to dip in anchovy-flavored mayonnaise, or simply with caviar for a gastronomic treat.

10oz mushrooms of your choice (e.g. portobello, chestnut, shiitake, oyster, or trompettes)

3 tablespoons virgin olive oil

2 garlic cloves *crushed*

sea salt (or kosher salt) and freshly ground black pepper

1 ball buffalo mozzarella *thinly sliced*

2 small ciabatta rolls *cut in half horizontally*

1 teaspoon freshly picked thyme leaves

oven-roasted mushrooms with mozzarella bread

Roasting the mushrooms with a little garlic and thyme really brings out their flavor. If you can't find an interesting selection of mushrooms, choose a single favorite variety instead.

1 Preheat the oven to 425°F.

2 Clean the mushrooms, slice thickly, then place in a roasting pan. Spoon 2 tablespoons of the olive oil over them, add the garlic, season with salt and pepper, and mix well. Place the mushrooms in the hot oven to roast for 15–20 minutes, until golden and tender.

3 Meanwhile, lay overlapping slices of mozzarella on the ciabatta halves, drizzle some of the remaining olive oil over them and sprinkle the thyme on top. Place on a baking tray and bake until golden and crispy and the cheese is melting.

4 To serve, cut the ciabatta into thick fingers and arrange around the mushrooms in a serving dish.

2 tablespoons virgin olive oil

4 canned anchovy fillets *rinsed, dried and finely chopped*

1 garlic clove *crushed*

2 tablespoons crushed walnuts

1 tablespoon white wine vinegar

3 tablespoons unsalted butter

zest of ½ lemon

2 tablespoons chopped flat-leaf parsley

1 cup fresh white bread crumbs *lightly toasted*

16 green asparagus tips

sea salt (or kosher salt)

asparagus with toasted anchovy gremolata

The classic Italian gremolata consists simply of garlic, parsley, and grated lemon. The addition of some anchovy and walnuts makes a fantastic topping for the lightly poached asparagus. And try adding an oozingly soft poached egg to the dish, too—delicious!

1 Heat the olive oil in a nonstick frying pan, add the anchovies and heat until softened. Add the garlic and walnuts and cook for 1 minute, then pour in the vinegar.

2 Add the butter to the pan and wait for it to start foaming before adding the lemon zest, parsley, and bread crumbs. Keep warm.

3 Cook the asparagus tips in boiling salted water for 2–3 minutes, then drain.

4 Arrange the asparagus on a dish and scatter the gremolata over it.

2 tablespoons virgin olive oil

1 garlic clove *crushed*

14oz small zucchini *cut at an angle into ½-inch slices*

2 tablespoons red wine vinegar

2 tablespoons honey

3 tablespoons currants

sea salt (or kosher salt) and freshly ground black pepper

1 teaspoon superfine capers *well rinsed*

3 tablespoons slivered almonds *toasted*

sweet and sour zucchini

The Italians really know how to cook vegetables, and make them taste out of this world. Here's a simple dish I first encountered in Venice.

1 Heat the oil in a large frying pan, add the garlic, and fry over a medium heat until the garlic is just beginning to color.

2 Throw in the zucchini slices and cook for 3–4 minutes, until lightly colored all over. Pour in the vinegar and honey, then add the currants.

3 Cover the pan with a lid and cook for 4–5 minutes, stirring occasionally.

4 Transfer the zucchini to a dish, to be served either warm or at room temperature. Before serving, season to taste, add the capers, and scatter the slivered almonds over them.

12 large cherry tomatoes

1 teaspoon sugar

1 garlic clove *crushed*

½ teaspoon freshly picked oregano
leaves

sea salt (or kosher salt) and freshly
ground black pepper

virgin olive oil

11½oz puff pastry dough

4oz firm, matured goat cheese *cut
into small pieces*

1 small pear *peeled and thinly shaved
for serving*

for the black oil

6 tablespoons virgin olive oil

8 black olives

goat cheese tarts with black oil

The slow roasting of the little tomatoes really brings out their natural sweetness
and accentuates their flavor.

1 Preheat the oven to 425°F.

2 Cut the cherry tomatoes in half and arrange on a foil-lined baking sheet.
Sprinkle them with the sugar, garlic, oregano, some salt, and a drizzle of
olive oil.

3 Place in the oven to slow roast for 30 minutes, by which time the tomatoes
should be soft and wilted but not mushy. Remove from the oven and let cool.

4 To make the black oil, simply blend the olive oil and olives in a small blender
until the olives are finely chopped.

5 Roll out the pastry dough to $^1/_8$-inch thick, then cut out twelve 3-inch circles
using a fluted cookie cutter. Prick each pastry circle with a fork and top with
roasted tomatoes (cut side up).

6 Transfer to a baking tray and place in the oven for 8–10 minutes, until the tarts
are nearly cooked. Scatter the cut up goat cheese over them and return to the
oven for another 2 minutes.

7 Remove and let cool. Before serving, drizzle with the black oil and top with
shavings of the thinly sliced pear.

14oz pork belly *cut into 2-inch pieces*
4oz pork fat back *cut into 2-inch pieces*
²/₃ cup dry white wine
2 garlic cloves
1 bay leaf
4 sprigs of thyme
pinch of mace
**sea salt (or kosher salt) and freshly
  ground black pepper**
a little flour
2 eggs *beaten*
**1¼ cups dried and fine white bread
  crumbs**
vegetable oil *for frying*

for the sauce
¹/₃ cup vinaigrette dressing
**1 chopped tablespoon each of: capers,
  gherkins, shallot, hard-boiled egg,
  and flat-leaf parsley**

crispy pork rillettes

Pork rillettes are one of the triumphs of classic French cooking, and are simple to prepare, if a little time-consuming. If time is of the essence, you could buy the rillettes from a deli; just make sure that they are of excellent quality.

1 Preheat the oven to 300°F.
2 Mix together all the ingredients for the rillettes (from pork belly down to salt and pepper) in a heavy casserole dish. Cover with a tight-fitting lid and cook in the oven for 3–4 hours, or until the meat is falling apart. Let cool. Remove the bay leaf and thyme sprigs.
3 Lift the pork meat out of the pan and roughly shred using two forks. Return the meat to the pork fat and pan juices, season to taste, and mix to combine. Pack into a small terrine or loaf pan and leave overnight in the fridge.
4 Remove the rillettes from the terrine and cut into roughly ½-inch cubes. Dip in the flour, the egg, and then in the bread crumbs.
5 Heat the oil in a frying pan and fry the breaded cubes until golden and crispy.
6 Make the sauce by mixing all the ingredients together and serve with the crispy rillettes.

1 large jar preserved baby artichokes
2 garlic cloves *crushed*
a handful of fresh basil leaves
2 tablespoons freshly grated Parmesan
1 tablespoon pine nuts
pinch of sugar
**sea salt (or kosher salt) and freshly
  ground black pepper**
juice of ½ lemon

artichokes in their own sauce

I first created artichoke pesto some years ago, as part of a pasta dish for a competition. It evolved into a sauce to serve with marinated artichokes—a surprising combination that has proved very popular among both vegetarians and meat-eaters.

1 Drain the artichokes, reserving the oil. Place a quarter of them in a small blender and mix to a coarse puree. Add the garlic, basil, Parmesan, pine nuts, and sugar, and blend again.
2 With the motor running, drizzle in the artichoke oil through the feeder tube to form a pesto-like sauce. Season and add lemon juice to taste.
3 Place the remaining artichokes on a serving dish, pour the artichoke sauce over them, and serve.

halibut crudo

In Italy, fish or meat served *crudo* (i.e. "raw") is becoming as popular as ceviche in Mexico. I particularly love fish prepared in this way. The important thing to remember is that the fish must be super-fresh.

1 Using a thin and very sharp knife, cut the halibut fillet into 1/8-inch-thick slices. Place in a shallow dish and season well with salt and pepper.
2 In a bowl, whisk together the lemon juice and olive oil with some salt and pepper. Add the remaining ingredients, mix well, and pour it over the halibut. Cover and let it marinate in the fridge for 30 minutes.
3 Serve the fish slices with the delicious marinade poured over the top.

18oz very fresh halibut fillet *skinned and boned*
juice of 1 lemon
4 tablespoons virgin olive oil
sea salt (or kosher salt) and freshly ground black pepper
½ small red chile *seeded and finely chopped*
2 ripe firm tomatoes *seeded and cut into small pieces*
8 fresh basil leaves *roughly chopped*
6 black olives *pitted and chopped into small pieces*
1 teaspoon superfine capers *rinsed and dried*
3 red radishes *very thinly sliced*

salmon tartare on blinis

A great and classic appetizer, salmon tartare is also a good way to use up any trimmings of smoked salmon.

1 To make the batter for the blinis, sift the flours into a bowl, add the baking powder, then stir in the egg, buttermilk (or milk), and melted butter. Stir until smooth then let rest for 15 minutes.
2 Heat the oil in a pan, add the fennel and fennel seeds, and cook over a low heat for 15–20 minutes, until tender and caramelized.
3 Place the salmon in a bowl, add the dill, salt, and pepper.
4 Melt about half a tablespoon of butter in a small nonstick frying pan. Drop tablespoons of batter into the pan in batches, cooking the blinis until golden on each side. Remove and keep warm.
5 To serve, place a little of the fennel mixture on each blini, followed by a spoonful of cream cheese, and top with the salmon.

2 tablespoons virgin olive oil
1 head fennel *very thinly sliced*
½ teaspoon fennel seeds
4oz smoked salmon *finely chopped*
2 tablespoons fresh dill *chopped*
sea salt (or kosher salt) and freshly ground black pepper
2 tablespoons cream cheese

for the blinis (makes 12–16)
6 tablespoons buckwheat flour
3 tablespoons all-purpose flour
½ teaspoon baking powder
1 egg *beaten*
½ cup buttermilk or milk
1½ tablespoons unsalted butter *melted*
extra butter *for frying*

goat cheese in provençal oil

4 firm goat cheeses (or one log cut into 4 sections)
2oz sunblush or sundried tomatoes in oil *drained*
1 teaspoon black peppercorns
4 garlic cloves *peeled and thinly sliced*
4 small bay leaves
4 sprigs rosemary
4 sprigs thyme
4 fresh or dried lavender sprigs
$^2/_3$ cup virgin olive oil

Quite recently, I started giving these goat cheeses in oil to guests as soon as they arrived in my restaurant, to whet their appetite. They have been a great success, and guests regularly ask for more as a starter to their meal. Thin slices of toasted walnut bread go superbly with the melting cheese, but warm baguette or focaccia bread is good, too.

1 Place each goat cheese inside a small canning jar. Divide the tomatoes, spices and herbs equally between the four jars, then add a sprig of lavender to each jar, too. Cover each cheese with olive oil.
2 Seal down the lids and keep refrigerated for one week prior to use.
3 When ready to serve, preheat the oven to 250°F. Place the jars in a roasting pan with an inch of water in the bottom and heat in the oven for 30 minutes, after which time the cheese should be warm and slightly softened in texture.
4 Let your guests enjoy eating the cheese straight from the jars.

chili-roasted fries with sour cream

4 large baking potatoes (e.g. russet)
$^1/_3$ cup virgin olive oil
sea salt (or kosher salt)
1–2 teaspoons chili powder (or to taste)
sour cream *for serving*

Here's a dish of simplicity if ever there was one. The potatoes can be replaced with sweet potatoes for a nice change.

1 Preheat the oven to 425°F.
2 Cut each potato into eight wedges and place in a bowl. Add the olive oil, salt, and chili powder, and toss until evenly coated.
3 Transfer to a baking sheet, cook for 15–20 minutes, turn them over and cook for another 15–20 minutes. Turn the potatoes again and continue cooking for a final 20 minutes, turning them until crisp and golden.
4 Cool slightly before serving with a dip of sour cream.

deviled whitebait (smelts)

14oz fresh whitebait (smelts)

sea salt (or kosher salt) and freshly
  ground black pepper

vegetable oil *for deep-frying*

4 tablespoons milk

2 tablespoons flour

cayenne pepper

lemon wedges *for serving*

I am so pleased to include this recipe in the book. These crispy little fishes, lightly devil-spiced with cayenne pepper, were one of the first dishes I ever prepared as a trainee chef at catering college many years ago.

1 Rinse the whitebait in cold water, drain, and dry well. Season the fish with salt and pepper.
2 Heat the vegetable oil to 325°F.
3 Dip the fish into the milk, drain, dip straight into the flour, then deep-fry until golden and crispy; this should take only 1–2 minutes. Drain on crumpled newspaper or paper towels.
4 Dust lightly with cayenne pepper, garnish with lemon wedges, and serve.

pg tip Crumpling up paper towels before using it to drain fried food allows the oil to be drained off more thoroughly. Newspaper works just as well as paper towels.

stuffed sardines with celery-leaf pesto

8 medium-size fresh sardines *cleaned*

2 tablespoons virgin olive oil

for the stuffing

1 tablespoon virgin olive oil

1 cup fresh white bread crumbs

2 tablespoons raisins *soaked in water
  for 20 minutes, then dried and chopped*

2 hard-boiled eggs *chopped*

sea salt (or kosher salt) and freshly
  ground black pepper

for the pesto

1¾oz celery leaf (as green as possible)

1oz flat-leaf parsley

1 garlic clove *crushed*

¼ cup pine nuts *lightly toasted*

⅓ cup virgin olive oil

Celery leaves usually get banished to the cheese tray, as garnish, or thrown into a stock or sauce. What a waste! Use them to create this unusual pesto to serve with sardines.

1 Preheat the oven to 400°F.
2 For the stuffing, heat the olive oil in a nonstick frying pan, add the bread crumbs, and fry until lightly golden in color. Transfer to a bowl and let cool. Add the raisins, eggs, and season to taste.
3 Cut the heads off the sardines, open them up by slitting along the belly with a knife, and carefully remove the inner spines. Wash the inside and pat dry.
4 Stuff the sardines with the stuffing, pressing the sides together, then place in a baking dish. Season with salt and pepper, drizzle the remaining oil over them, then bake in the hot oven for 10–12 minutes.
5 Meanwhile mix the celery leaf, parsley, garlic, and pine nuts in a blender. Add the olive oil to form a light sauce, and season to taste.
6 Transfer the sardines to a serving dish, drizzle the pesto over them, and serve.

cherry tomato and bocconcini lollipops

12 **cherry tomatoes** *stems removed*
1 tablespoon **tapenade**
12 *bocconcini* **(baby mozzarella)**
½ teaspoon **grated lemon zest**
2 tablespoons **virgin olive oil**
1 tablespoon **chopped flat-leaf parsley**

A simple but eye-catching recipe based on the Caprese salad, Italy's ubiquitous pairing of mozzarella and tomato.

1 With a sharp knife, remove the top ½ inch of each tomato. Using a melon baller, scoop out the seeds of each one, ensuring that the outer "shell" is left intact.

2 Spoon a little tapenade into the bottom of each tomato, followed by one of the baby *bocconcini*.

3 Skewer the bottom of each tomato with a large wooden or bamboo skewer. For the most eye-catching presentation, stand the lollipops in tall glasses.

4 In a bowl, combine the lemon zest, olive oil, and parsley. Drizzle a little over each tomato before serving.

porcini croquettes

3½ tablespoons **unsalted butter**
3oz **flour (plus a little extra for rolling)**
1¾ cups **milk**
2 tablespoons **virgin olive oil**
7oz **fresh porcini mushrooms (or any cultivated mushroom)** *roughly chopped*
1 large **shallot** *finely chopped*
1 small **garlic clove** *crushed*
sea salt (or kosher salt) and freshly ground black pepper
2 **eggs** *beaten*
1⅔ cups **dry white bread crumbs**
virgin olive oil *for deep-frying*

Porcini (or cèpe) are a variety of *Boletus* mushroom. The name originates from the Latin word *bolet*, meaning "superior mushroom," which is exactly what porcini are. They have a distinct aroma, reminiscent of fermented dough.

1 First, make your white sauce. Melt the butter in a pan, sprinkle in the flour, and beat until smooth, cooking over a low heat to form a classic roux. Add the milk a little at a time, ensuring each addition is combined with the roux before adding more. Cook over a low heat for 5–8 minutes until the sauce is smooth, satin-like in appearance, and very thick in consistency. Set aside.

2 Heat the olive oil in a frying pan. When hot, add the roughly chopped mushrooms and cook for 2–3 minutes, until they are tender and golden. Add the shallot and garlic and cook for another 2 minutes.

3 Add the mushroom mixture to the white sauce, stir well, season to taste another and then transfer to a bowl to cool. Once cooled, transfer the mixture onto a lightly floured surface and shape into a long roll about ¾ inch in diameter. Cut into 1¼-inch sections.

4 Coat each formed croquette with the egg and bread crumbs. (These uncooked croquettes can be chilled until needed.)

5 When ready to serve, heat the olive oil to 325°F in a deep frying pan and fry the croquettes a few at a time for 2–3 minutes, until heated through and golden.

4 slices prosciutto *cut in half*

8 small sage leaves (plus extra, for garnishing)

2 tablespoons *mostarda di Cremona* (Italian mustard fruits), *chopped*

12oz monkfish (angler fish) fillet *skinned, boned, and cut into 8 cubes*

sea salt (or kosher salt) and freshly ground black pepper

3 tablespoons virgin olive oil

2 tablespoons unsalted butter

zest of ½ lemon

1 teaspoon balsamic vinegar

monkfish spiedini with mustard fruits

A *spiedino* is the name of a kabob in Italian. The idea to use prosciutto and sage to wrap around the monkfish comes from the classic Italian dish *saltimbocca*, though this traditionally uses veal rather than fish.

1 Lay out the half-slices of prosciutto on a counter. In the center of each, place a sage leaf, a little mustard fruit, and, lastly, a cube of monkfish. Season lightly with salt and pepper. Wrap the prosciutto around the fish to form a wrap, securing each with a toothpick or skewer.

2 Heat 2 tablespoons olive oil in a frying pan. When hot, add the wraps and fry for 2–3 minutes on each side, until golden and tender. Remove and keep warm on a serving dish.

3 Clean the pan with paper towels and return to the heat. Add the butter and heat until it foams up, then add the lemon zest and the vinegar. Let the sauce bubble for 30 seconds.

4 Heat the remaining tablespoon of olive oil in a pan, and fry a handful of sage leaves for about 30 seconds, until crisp. Drain on paper towels.

5 Pour the sauce over the fish wraps, scatter the fried sage leaves on top, and serve immediately.

pg tip Italian mustard fruits, known in Italy as *mostarda di Cremona* or *mostarda di frutta*, are candied fruits preserved in a sweet, mustard-flavored syrup. They go beautifully with sausages, cold meats, and cheese. You'll find them in Italian delis.

piggyback dates on polenta

12 Medjool dates *pitted*
2oz Gorgonzola cheese *lightly crumbled*
6 slices of bacon

for the polenta squares
²/₃ cup quick-cook polenta (cornmeal)
5 teaspoons unsalted butter
2 tablespoons grated Parmesan
2 tablespoons virgin olive oil

Medjool dates are the best dates you can buy: sweet, sticky, out of this world... In contrast, the bacon and cheese add some necessary saltiness, making one hell of a canapé.

1 To prepare the polenta squares, bring 3 cups water to the boil in a pan and then gradually add the polenta, stirring constantly until it acquires a porridge-like consistency. Reduce the heat to low and cook for 10–12 minutes, until the polenta is very thick.

2 Add the Parmesan and butter, then spread into a shallow, well-greased 8-inch baking tray. Refrigerate overnight, covered in plastic wrap.

3 The next day, cut the dates lengthwise across the top, without cutting right through. Open them up as far as you can. Fill each date with Gorgonzola, then wrap in a half-slice of bacon, spearing each with a toothpick.

4 Heat a grill pan until very hot and brush with olive oil.

5 Cut the polenta into twelve 2-inch diamonds. Place on the grill and cook until golden on both sides. At the same time, grill the dates until the bacon is crispy.

6 Serve the dates on top of the grilled polenta diamonds.

chicken liver bruschetta with balsamic figs

10oz fresh chicken livers *(frozen livers are fine but must be fully defrosted)*
¹/₃ cup milk
3 tablespoons virgin olive oil
sea salt (or kosher salt) and freshly ground black pepper
¼ teaspoon fennel seeds
4 tablespoons balsamic vinegar
4 ripe but firm figs *cut into wedges*
8 slices French bread *(or sourdough)*

Figs and balsamic vinegar work so well together, and the combination of the sweet fruit and tart vinegar is the perfect foil for the rich chicken livers. A little arugula goes nicely with this dish, adding an extra peppery bite.

1 Cut the liver into bite-size pieces, remove any traces of green bile, then place in a bowl. Pour the milk over them and let soak for 30 minutes (this helps to remove any bitterness).

2 Remove the livers from the milk, quickly rinse in cold water, then dry them well.

3 Heat the olive oil in a nonstick frying pan. Once the oil is hot, season the livers with salt, pepper, and the fennel seeds, and add to the pan. Fry over a high heat for about 1 minute.

4 Pour in the vinegar and let it bubble for a while. Add the figs and toss with the liver pieces until they are all well coated in glaze (making sure that the livers stay pink in the center).

5 To serve, toast the bread slices until golden, pile the glazed livers on top, and drizzle any remaining pan juices over them.

1²/₃ cups flour

pinch of salt

1 x ¼-oz (7g) sachet envelope
  rapid-rise yeast

8 salted anchovy fillets *cut in half,
  rinsed, and dried*

2oz (about ½ cup) Gorgonzola cheese
  crumbled

vegetable oil *for frying*

zeppole with anchovy and gorgonzola

These doughnut-like pastries, eaten mainly in Calabria and other parts of southern Italy, are normally filled with a sweet cream. This version, however, is savory, made with one of Italy's greatest cheeses.

1 Sift the flour into a bowl. Add the salt and yeast, then make a well in the center. Pour in ²/₃ cup warm water and bring the ingredients together to form a soft, pliable dough. Place in a lightly oiled bowl, cover with plastic wrap, and leave in the fridge for 2 hours.

2 Transfer the dough to a work surface and punch it down, kneading for about a minute.

3 Divide the dough into 16 small balls. Flatten each one on the palm of your hand, place a piece of anchovy and some Gorgonzola in the center, and fold over the dough to secure the filling. Flatten lightly with the other hand, stretching the dough as you do so.

4 Heat a frying pan with an inch of oil in the bottom. When hot, cook the *zeppole* in batches until golden. Drain on paper towels and serve.

½ cup virgin olive oil

18oz pork belly *cut into small cubes*

1 tablespoon smoked paprika

2 onions *peeled and chopped*

1 garlic clove *crushed*

2½oz bacon *cut into small pieces*

3 red peppers *seeded and cut into strips*

3 firm tomatoes *blanched, peeled, and
  seeded*

1 tablespoon freshly chopped flat-leaf
  parsley

1 tablespoon freshly chopped cilantro

1 small red chile *finely chopped*

14oz clams or cockles

cataplana

Many of you may have eaten this pork and shellfish stew while on vacation in Portugal. The word *cataplana* is actually the name of the dish that the stew is cooked and served in. But, never fear, any large heavy pan with a lid will do the job fine.

1 Heat the olive oil in a heavy pan. When hot, add the pork and paprika and fry for 5–6 minutes, until the meat is crispy all over.

2 Add the onions, garlic, bacon, and peppers, and sauté for another 5 minutes. Then add the tomatoes, herbs, and chile. Reduce the heat and let cook gently, covered, for 5–6 minutes.

3 Finally, add the clams, mix well, and cook, covered, over a low heat for 5 minutes. Transfer to deep soup bowls when ready to serve.

¼ small English cucumber *seeded and cut into small pieces*

1 small red onion *thinly sliced*

2 tomatoes *cut into small pieces*

½ teaspoon dried oregano

2 tablespoons red wine vinegar

4 tablespoons virgin olive oil

2½oz (about ½ cup) feta cheese

1 garlic clove *crushed*

8 black olives *pitted and finely chopped*

4 pita breads

4½oz (about 1⅓ cups) cheddar cheese

greek-style quesadillas

Feta cheese, the key ingredient in this simple recipe, is a great cheese to serve as an appetizer, its saltiness working wonders with an apéritif.

1 In a bowl, combine the cucumber, onion, tomatoes, oregano, vinegar, and 2 tablespoons of the olive oil. Let stand for 20 minutes, then drain thoroughly.

2 Crush the feta cheese in a bowl with the garlic and olives. Cut the pitas in half, horizontally to give you eight circles, then spread the tops of four circles with the feta mixture.

3 Divide the salad over these four circles, sprinkle the cheddar on top, then cover with the remaining pita circles to form sandwiches.

4 Heat the remaining oil in a large nonstick frying pan over a medium heat, and cook the "quesadillas" until the cheese melts, about 2–3 minutes per side. Cut into wedges when ready to serve.

pg tip Always choose a good-quality feta, which traditionally is a blend of 30 percent goat's milk and 70 percent sheep's milk. Avoid the cheap, poorly produced versions.

north africa
and the middle east

From Turkey to Tunisia, mezze are one of the most enchanting traditions of this region—a glorious array of little dishes that can start or make a meal.

Spice market in Aswan, Egypt

1 onion *peeled and cut into quarters*
good pinch of saffron threads
14oz cooked chickpeas (the canned
  variety is fine) *drained*
1/3 cup tahini
1/2 teaspoon ground cumin
pinch of cayenne pepper
2 garlic cloves *crushed*
sea salt (or kosher salt) and freshly
  ground black pepper
2 tablespoons virgin olive oil

moroccan-style hummus

In my opinion, there's no better way to prepare hummus. It's such a great dip, and a wonderful spread for vegetarian sandwiches.

1 Place the onion in a small pan with the saffron and 2 tablespoons of water. Cover with a lid and cook gently for 10 minutes, until the onion is tender. Drain into a colander and let cool.

2 Place the onion and all the remaining ingredients (except the olive oil) in a blender or food processor and blend to a smooth puree, adding a little more water if necessary. Season to taste.

3 Transfer to a serving dish, drizzle the olive oil over it, and serve with lots of toasted Middle Eastern-style flatbread.

1 teaspoon caraway seeds
1/2 teaspoon cumin seeds
14oz (about 1¾ cups) freshly
  ground lamb
1 onion *grated*
1 garlic clove *crushed*
1/2 teaspoon paprika
2 tablespoons freshly chopped mint
6 black olives *pitted and finely chopped*

for the sauce
a good 1/2 cup blanched almonds
1 slice white bread *cut into small pieces*
3 tablespoons virgin olive oil
good pinch of saffron threads
1 tablespoon tahini
3 cups chicken stock
2 tablespoons vegetable oil

turkish lamb kofta in tchina sauce

The sauce served with these spicy lamb meatballs is simply the African version of tahini.

Note: You need to prepare the koftas the day before you plan to eat them.

1 To prepare the koftas, place a small dry frying pan on a high heat, add the caraway and cumin seeds, and toast until fragrant, about 15 seconds. Shake the pan constantly to prevent the spices from burning. Place in a spice blender or mortar and crush to a fine powder.

2 Transfer the crushed spices to a bowl, then add the lamb and the remaining kofta ingredients. Mix well but do not overwork.

3 Using wet hands, divide the mixture into small balls about an inch in diameter. Refrigerate overnight on a plate, covered with plastic wrap.

4 To make the sauce, fry the almonds and bread pieces in the olive oil until golden in color. Transfer to a blender or food processor, add the saffron, tahini, and ¾ cup of the chicken stock, and blitz to a smooth sauce.

5 Heat the oil in a heavy pan, add the meatballs and fry each side to seal all over, until golden. Add the saffron sauce and remaining stock, bring to a boil, and simmer very gently for 20 minutes, until the meatballs are cooked through. Thin the sauce with a little water if necessary.

6 Transfer the kofta to a serving dish and pour the sauce over them.

10oz (about 1¼ cups) lean ground
 beef or lamb
½ cup cooked rice
sea salt (or kosher salt) and freshly
 ground black pepper
1 small onion *finely chopped*
2 tablespoons chopped flat-leaf parsley
½ teaspoon dried mint
1 teaspoon ground cardamom
1 tablespoon plain yogurt
1 teaspoon virgin olive oil
2 eggs
a little flour
3½ tablespoons unsalted butter

kadin budu

These twice-cooked meatballs are popular throughout Syria. The recipe,
particularly the type of meat, varies from town to town: some prefer lamb,
others beef.

1 Place the meat in a bowl with the rice, salt and pepper, onion, parsley, dried
 mint, cardamom, yogurt, olive oil, and one of the eggs. Mix together to form a
 smooth paste.
2 Using wet hands, divide the mixture into around 20–25 balls the size of a small
 golf ball, then flatten each one a little in the palm of your hand.
3 Place the meatballs in a pan and just cover with boiling water. Reduce the heat
 to a simmer and cook for 10 minutes. Drain and let cool.
4 Beat the remaining egg, dip the meatballs in it, then roll them in the flour. Heat
 the butter in a frying pan, add the balls, and fry until crisp and brown.

2½oz fresh raw spinach leaves (1½ large
 handfuls) *cooked and chopped*
1 red chile *seeded and finely chopped*
1 garlic clove *crushed*
zest of ½ lemon
1½ cups cooked chickpeas *mashed
 with a fork*
1²⁄₃ cups chickpea flour (gram flour)
1 teaspoon baking powder
2½oz (about ½ cup) feta cheese
 crumbled
3 eggs
a handful of fresh cilantro leaves
 chopped
vegetable oil *for deep-frying*

for the beet tzatziki
2oz cooked beets *finely chopped or
 grated*
4 tablespoons plain yogurt
1 tablespoon freshly chopped mint

chickpea and spinach fritters with beet tzatziki

These light and fluffy fritters are beautifully simple to make, and nutritious, too.
The beet tzatziki adds a touch of elegance alongside them.

1 Put all the ingredients for the fritters (excluding the oil) in a bowl. Mix together
 well, then let chill for 1 hour in the fridge.
2 For the tzatziki, mix the ingredients together in a bowl and season to taste.
3 Heat the oil in a large, deep pan to 325°F. Drop in walnut-sized spoonfuls of the
 fritter mixture, and fry until golden.
4 Drain on paper towels and serve immediately with the beet tzatziki.

14oz chicken thighs *skinned, boned, and cut into 1-inch pieces*

sea salt (or kosher salt) and freshly ground black pepper

1 tablespoon paprika

2 garlic cloves *crushed*

4 tablespoons plain yogurt

juice of ½ lemon

2 tablespoons vegetable oil

2 flour tortillas

4 tablespoons garlic mayonnaise (see aïoli recipe on page 59)

½ small red onion *finely sliced*

1 firm ripe tomato *roughly chopped*

shish taouk wraps

There are as many marinade recipes as there are cooks. Here's one of the simplest and one of my favorites, inspired by Lebanon's *shish taouk*, grilled garlic chicken. The yogurt really tenderizes the meat beautifully, while the garlic and paprika add an all-encompassing flavor.

1 Place the thigh pieces in a bowl and season well with salt and pepper. Add the paprika, garlic, yogurt, and lemon juice, and mix together well. Cover with plastic wrap and refrigerate overnight.

2 To serve, remove the chicken from the marinade and dry off any excess. Thread the pieces onto four barbecue skewers.

3 Heat a grill pan and brush it liberally with oil. Cook the skewers on the grill for 6–8 minutes, turning them regularly until cooked and lightly charred.

4 Place the flour tortillas on the grill for 1 minute on each side to reheat them.

5 Spread a little garlic mayonnaise onto each tortilla, add some meat down the center, and then top off with some onion and tomato. Wrap the tortilla tightly to secure the filling. Cut each tortilla in half when ready to serve.

pg tip Paprika as a seasoning seems to be making a culinary comeback. There are some great ones available, Hungarian probably being the most sought after. Spanish paprika is good, too, including *picante pimentón*, Spain's wonderful smoked paprika.

lebanese chicken wings

⅓ cup plus 2 tablespoons virgin olive oil
good handful of cilantro, leaves only
juice of 2½ lemons
2 garlic cloves *crushed*
2 tablespoons maple syrup
1 teaspoon ground cumin
½ teaspoon ground coriander
¼ teaspoon ground cayenne pepper
½ teaspoon sumac
12 large chicken wings
2 tablespoons vegetable oil

Chicken wings are very cheap, and really do make a good tidbit for canapés and the like. Most butchers now sell them due to the growing demand.

1 In a blender, combine the olive oil, cilantro, juice of 2 lemons, garlic, maple syrup, dried spices and sumac, and blitz until smooth. Transfer to a bowl.

2 Make three slashes in the meaty part of each chicken wing, add to the marinade, and toss well. Marinate for 4 hours at room temperature.

3 Preheat a ridged grill pan. Meanwhile, thread the wings onto four wooden or bamboo skewers, reserving the marinade. Brush the wings with vegetable oil, place on the very hot grill, and cook for 4–5 minutes, or until the wings are crispy and caramelized in appearance. Baste the chicken with the reserved marinade occasionally as they cook.

4 Transfer to a serving dish and squeeze over the juice from the last half lemon over them.

4 x 4-oz fresh salmon trout (or steelhead
  trout) fillets, with the skin on
sea salt (or kosher salt)
smoked paprika

for the chermoula
4 tablespoons virgin olive oil
good pinch of powdered saffron (or
  turmeric)
1 garlic clove *crushed*
½ teaspoon ground cumin
2 tablespoons freshly chopped mint
1 tablespoon flat-leaf parsley
juice of 1 lemon
sea salt (or kosher salt) and freshly
  ground black pepper

paprika salmon trout with mint chermoula

I love the colors in this dish—they are amazingly appealing to both the eye and
the palate. Regular salmon is fine if you can't get hold of the trout but hold out
for the latter if you can as it combines the qualities of both these delicious fish.

1 Make several slashes across the skin of the salmon trout fillets. Season them
  liberally with salt and smoked paprika, using your hands to push the seasoning
  into the cut slats in the fish. Let them marinate for 1 hour.
2 Meanwhile, make the chermoula. Place the olive oil and saffron together in a
  small pan over a low heat for 5–8 minutes. Remove and let cool.
3 Mix the remaining chermoula ingredients in a bowl, add the saffron oil, and
  season to taste.
4 Grill the fish on a preheated hot grill pan for 3–4 minutes on each side. Coat
  with the chermoula and serve.

1½ cups fresh white bread crumbs
12 small chicken drumsticks *skinned*
1 tablespoon Dijon mustard
a little flour
2 egg whites *lightly beaten*

for the dukka
⅓ cup finely chopped almonds
2½ tablespoons sesame seeds
3 tablespoons coriander seeds
2 teaspoons cumin seeds
sea salt (or kosher salt) and freshly
  ground black pepper

dukka-crumbed drumsticks

Dukka is an Egyptian spice mix that is simply delicious. The more you eat, the
more addictive it becomes. Sprinkle it on crusty bread drizzled with olive oil, or
use it to coat chicken, as in this recipe. If you're wondering what to serve with
the drumsticks, small crisp French fries fit the bill perfectly.

1 For the *dukka*, heat a dry frying pan and, when hot, add the almonds and seeds.
  Toast for 30 seconds, stirring all the time. Crush in a mortar with some salt and
  pepper, but not too finely. Mix the *dukka* with the bread crumbs.
2 Brush the drumsticks liberally with the mustard. Dip them in the flour, in the
  beaten egg whites, and then, finally, in the *dukka* crumb mixture.
3 Preheat the oven to 400°F.
4 Place the chicken drumsticks in a single layer on a baking tray and bake for
  15–20 minutes, or until cooked and golden.

1½ cups frozen peas

375g dried chickpeas *soaked in cold water overnight*

2 scallions *finely chopped*

1 garlic clove *crushed*

1 teaspoon ground cumin

1 red chile *seeded and finely chopped*

2 tablespoons freshly chopped mint

1 cup white bread crumbs

1 egg

sea salt (or kosher salt) and freshly ground black pepper

2 tablespoons vegetable oil

pea and mint tameyas

Tameyas are, essentially, a type of Israeli falafel. The inclusion of peas gives a wonderful color and freshness to the patties. Chili-spiked yogurt would make a nice accompaniment.

1 Blanch the peas in boiling water for 1 minute, then drain well.
2 Drain the chickpeas thoroughly and blend in a food processor with the peas and remaining ingredients (except the oil) until smooth. Season to taste.
3 Roll the mixture into golf ball-size balls, flatten them into patties, and place on a tray. Cover and refrigerate for 1 hour.
4 When ready to serve, heat the oil in a frying pan and fry the patties until golden, 1–2 minutes per side. Drain on paper towels.

⅓ cup plus 2 tablespoons virgin olive oil

1 onion *finely chopped*

1 garlic clove *crushed*

2 x 6-oz chicken breasts *skinned, boned and chopped*

a little cinnamon

½ teaspoon sugar

pinch of saffron threads

½ cup raisins

⅓ cup peeled pistachios (optional)

1 package phyllo dough (or spring roll wrappers)

1 egg *beaten*

a little confectioners' sugar

chicken briouats

These crispy stuffed phyllo pastries, which usually come in a triangle or cigar shape, are one of the most popular street foods in Morocco. The light sprinkling of confectioners' sugar at the end is in keeping with the Moroccan penchant for adding a touch of sweetness to their savory dishes.

1 Heat 2 tablespoons of the olive oil in a frying pan. Add the onion and garlic and cook until softened and lightly golden.
2 Add the chopped chicken, cinnamon, sugar, saffron, raisins, and pistachios (if using), and fry lightly to infuse the meat with the aromatic spices. Cook for 8–10 minutes, then transfer to a bowl and let cool.
3 Remove 5 sheets of the phyllo dough from the package and keep them moist under a damp cloth. Cut each sheet into roughly eighteen squares, roughly 3 inches square.
4 Place a little of the cooled chicken mixture onto one corner of the phyllo square, then brush the edges with beaten egg. Fold the square over to make a triangle, pressing down to ensure the edges are firmly closed together. Brush liberally with beaten egg all over, then let them rest for 30 minutes.
5 Heat the rest of the olive oil to 325°F in a pan, and cook the pastries for 2–3 minutes, until golden. Remove, and dust liberally with confectioners' sugar.

4 tablespoons virgin olive oil

1 small eggplant *cut into ¼-inch cubes*

1 onion *finely chopped*

½ teaspoon ground cumin

sea salt (or kosher salt) and freshly
  ground black pepper

2 ripe firm tomatoes *cut into small cubes*

⅓ cup cooked spinach *chopped*

1 garlic clove *crushed*

½ teaspoon sumac

2 tablespoons pine nuts

12oz pie dough

a little beaten egg

12oz fresh mackerel (or red snapper)
  fillets *boned and cut into 2-inch lengths*

mackerel fatayer

Fatayer is the name of a small Lebanese pastry. In Lebanon, it is often stuffed with spinach, but almost any filling could be used. Ground lamb and feta go particularly well together, but here I use mackerel, which works beautifully, too. Try flavoring some yogurt with mint or sumac as an accompaniment.

1 Preheat the oven to 400°F.

2 Heat 3 tablespoons of the olive oil in a large frying pan, add the eggplant cubes, and fry for 8–10 minutes until golden. Add the onion and cumin and cook for another 2 minutes. Season to taste. Transfer the mixture to a bowl and let cool.

3 Heat the remaining oil in the pan and add the tomatoes, spinach, garlic, sumac, and pine nuts. Cook until almost dry in texture. Season to taste.

4 Roll out the dough to ⅛-inch thick and cut out twelve 3-inch circles using a cookie cutter. Brush the edges with the beaten egg.

5 Place a heaped spoonful of the eggplant mixture in the center of each circle, then top with a spoonful of the spinach and tomato mixture. Finally, top with a section of seasoned mackerel. Roll up the stuffed pastry, seal, then gently twist and press each end using your your thumb and index finger.

6 Place the pies on a greased baking sheet and brush the exterior surfaces with more beaten egg. Bake for 15–20 minutes until golden.

pg tip Sumac is a lemon-tasting red berry that is dried and ground, and used extensively in salads, and to flavor meat and fish dishes, throughout Lebanon, Syria, and Israel. It is available from Middle Eastern stores.

18oz baby octopus *heads and beaks removed, cleaned*
¼ cup virgin olive oil

for the zhoug
½ small onion *chopped*
2 garlic cloves *crushed*
1 teaspoon sugar
small bunch of fresh cilantro
½ teaspoon coriander seeds
½ teaspoon cumin seeds
3 green chiles *seeded and chopped*
scant cup virgin olive oil

charbroiled baby octopus with green zhoug

Baby octopus can be obtained from good fish markets, although there are also some good-quality frozen ones available. Failing that, you could use squid, cut into large pieces.

1 First, make the zhoug. Place the onion, garlic, sugar, and fresh cilantro into a small blender and mix briefly.

2 In a dry frying pan, toast the coriander and cumin seeds, along with the chopped green chiles, for 1 minute. Add to the blender and mix. Then, with the motor running, gradually add the olive oil through the feeder tube to form a thick relish-style sauce.

3 Place the octopus in a dish, pour the olive oil and the prepared zhoug over it and mix well together. Cover and refrigerate for 2 hours.

4 To serve, remove the octopus from its marinade and place on a preheated hot grill pan. Cook, turning regularly and brushing regularly with the reserved zhoug marinade, for 6–8 minutes, or until cooked.

pg tip Zhoug is a spicy chili sauce preparation from the Yemen made from green or red chiles. It is great in spreads, as a marinade, or added to salad dressings.

cumin-spiced pork with muhammara

for the pork

14oz pork tenderloin *cut into large cubes*

2 tablespoons virgin olive oil

2 tablespoons white wine vinegar

1 garlic clove *crushed*

1 teaspoon cumin seeds

1 teaspoon smoked paprika

for the muhammara

3 red peppers *roasted, peeled, and seeded*

¼ teaspoon red pepper flakes

scant cup walnuts

2 tablespoons *dibs rumen* **(pomegranate molasses)**

½ teaspoon ground cumin

2 tablespoons virgin olive oil (and a little extra for drizzling)

a little sugar

a little sea salt (or kosher salt)

½ tablespoon lemon juice

paprika *for dusting*

The odd-sounding *muhammara* is a traditional spice paste from the Yemen, not dissimilar to Tunisian harissa. If you like a little spice kick in your dip, look no further. The red pepper flakes add real "umph" to the *muhammara*, while the roasted peppers and molasses add a pleasingly smoky sweetness.

1 Marinate the pork cubes in the oil, vinegar, garlic, cumin seeds, and paprika overnight.

2 For the muhammara, place the peppers, red pepper flakes, walnuts, molasses, and cumin in a blender and puree to a smooth and creamy paste. Transfer to a bowl, beat in the olive oil, sugar, and salt, and finish with lemon juice to taste.

3 Divide the pork onto four presoaked wooden or bamboo skewers, and cook on a preheated hot grill pan or barbecue for 4–5 minutes, turning until golden and cooked through.

4 Spoon the muhammara onto a serving dish, drizzle a little olive oil over it and dust with paprika. Arrange the skewers on the bed of muhammara and serve.

pg tip Pomegranate molasses *(dibs rumen)* is a wonder syrup used widely in Middle Eastern cooking. It tastes fantastic added to meat stews, or when used to add a little sourness to braised dishes. It's well worth digging out a specialty store that sells it.

1 cup cracked wheat (or bulgur)

1 x 15oz can chickpeas *drained*

3 scallions *finely chopped*

3 tablespoons chopped fresh mint

2 tablespoons chopped flat-leaf parsley

juice of 2 lemons

1/3 cup virgin olive oil

1/2 teaspoon ground cinnamon

sea salt (or kosher salt) and freshly
ground black pepper

1 little gem (or romaine) lettuce *for
serving*

saffi

This Lebanese cracked wheat salad is one step up from the traditional tabbouleh. Try adding grilled shrimp or some other seafood to the finished salad.

1 Place the cracked wheat in a large bowl and add enough cold water to cover. Set aside for 15 minutes, then drain well, squeezing the grains between your hands to extract all the excess water. Return to the bowl.

2 Add the chickpeas and remaining ingredients (except the lettuce), season to taste, and toss well.

3 Serve with the little gem lettuce, whose sturdy leaves can be used to scoop up the saffi for eating.

14oz pork tenderloin *cut into 1-inch
cubes*

1/3 cup virgin olive oil

1 small onion *finely chopped*

1 garlic clove *crushed*

1 tablespoon chopped fresh mint (plus
some for garnishing)

1 tablespoon paprika

1/2 tablespoon ground cumin

juice of 1 lemon

country bread *for serving*

for the dip

1/2 cup plain yogurt

1/4 teaspoon ground cinnamon

1/4 teaspoon ground cumin

1/4 teaspoon ground ginger

sea salt (or kosher salt) and freshly
ground black pepper

moorish kabobs with a spicy dip

Kabobs were first introduced to Europe by Arabs from North Africa. They were made with lamb originally, but nowadays pork is often the preferred meat.

1 In a bowl, mix the meat with all the remaining ingredients, cover with plastic wrap, and marinate overnight, allowing time for you to turn the mixture occasionally.

2 When ready to serve, thread equal amounts of pork onto eight presoaked wooden or bamboo skewers. Place on a preheated grill pan and cook, turning regularly, until golden and cooked through.

3 Meanwhile, mix the dip ingredients together and season to taste.

4 Scatter the kabobs with the remaining mint and serve with the dip and large chunks of country bread.

4 tablespoons virgin olive oil

4 large (1lb–18oz) boneless quails
(available from specialty butchers)
skinned

1½ tablespoons unsalted butter (plus
extra for brushing the pastry)

1 onion *finely chopped*

1 teaspoon ground cardamom

good pinch of saffron threads

1 teaspoon ground cinnamon

½ cup ground walnuts

1 tablespoon chopped cilantro

1 tablespoon chopped flat-leaf parsley

8 sheets phyllo pastry dough

for the salsa

1 tablespoon olive oil

1 tablespoon lemon juice

1 tablespoon honey

1 cooked beet *peeled and cut into
½-inch cubes*

1 orange *peeled, flesh cut into
½-inch pieces*

1 small red onion *peeled and cut into
½-inch pieces*

6 green pitted olives *cut into
½-inch pieces*

2 tablespoons freshly chopped cilantro

quail baklava with beet, olive, and orange salsa

You're right, baklava is a classic Middle Eastern sweet made from honey, nuts and filo pastry. In typical PG style, however, I have created my own savory version, using young quails. I hope you agree that it tastes good.

1 Heat half of the olive oil in a nonstick frying pan. When hot, add the quails, fry quickly until golden, then remove.

2 Add the butter to the frying pan, along with the onion, cardamom, saffron, cinnamon, and walnuts, and cook over a low heat. Return the quails to the pan, mix with the spices and herbs, then cover the pan with a lid and cook gently for 5–6 minutes. Remove from the heat and transfer to a bowl to cool.

3 To make the baklava, brush the phyllo dough sheets liberally with melted butter, placing one on top of another. When you have used up all the sheets, cut the layered pastry in half vertically and horizontally to form four squares.

4 Place one quail and some of the filling in the center of each square, then bring the four edges up to seal the quail in the center. Turn the baklava over and place it on a plate. Prepare the other three in the same way, then let them rest for 30 minutes in the fridge.

5 Meanwhile, make the salsa. Simply mix all the ingredients together in a bowl, then let it marinate for 30 minutes.

6 When ready to serve, heat the remaining oil in a nonstick frying pan, add the baklavas, and cook over a medium heat for 3–4 minutes on each side, until golden and crispy.

**½lb (about 1½–2 cups) boiled new
   potatoes** *peeled*
1 cup feta cheese *crumbled*
2 tablespoons chopped fresh mint
**sea salt (or kosher salt) and freshly
   ground black pepper**
6 sheets phyllo pastry dough
3 tablespoons virgin olive oil

potato, feta, and mint tiropites

The beauty of these little pastries is that they freeze extremely well (uncooked), for up to one month. Replacing the potato with eggplant or peppers tastes equally good.

1 Preheat the oven to 425°F.
2 Dry the hot peeled potatoes in a dry pan over a low heat. Roughly mash them, then remove from the pan and let cool.
3 Stir in the crumbled feta cheese and mint, and season to taste.
4 While assembling the tiropites, keep the phyllo dough sheets covered with a damp cloth. Working on one sheet of dough at a time, brush the phyllo lightly with some olive oil, then cut it into three long strips.
5 Place 1 tablespoon of filling at the top of one phyllo strip. Fold the corner of the phyllo over the filling, so that the top edge of the pastry dough is now over the right edge. Take the point of the strip and fold this down towards the bottom of the pastry dough. Continue to fold this way to make a pastry-filled triangle. Repeat with the other strips, followed by the other sheets.
6 Transfer the turnovers to baking trays and brush with the remaining oil.
7 Cook at the top of the oven for 18–20 minutes, until crisp and golden. Serve warm.

¼ cup virgin olive oil

8 medium-size fresh sardines *scaled, gutted, and butterflied (head removed)*

coarse sea salt (or kosher salt)

4 garlic cloves *crushed*

a pinch of saffron threads

1 tablespoon smoked paprika

2 bay leaves

12 black olives *pitted*

2 Lebanese pickled chiles (or 1 small red or green chile, chopped) *shredded finely*

pinch of sugar

⅓ cup white wine vinegar

sardines with pickled chile and olives

My take on a Spanish *escabeche* uses Lebanese pickled chiles and saffron as the dominant flavorings. Any type of oily fish, including mullet or mackerel, works well.

1 First prepare the sardines for marinating. Starting from the head end, roll up each sardine tightly, and secure by piercing a toothpick through the tail.

2 Heat the olive oil in a nonstick frying pan, season the sardines with sea salt, and fry them on both sides for 2–3 minutes. Transfer to a shallow dish.

3 Strain the oil used for cooking the sardines and clean the frying pan. Return that oil to the pan, add the garlic, saffron, and paprika, and fry gently for 1 minute. Add the bay leaves, olives, chiles, sugar, and wine vinegar, along with a scant ½ cup water. Simmer gently for 2 minutes.

4 Pour the liquid over the sardines and let them marinate for 3–4 hours, to allow the flavors to infuse into the fish.

5 Serve at room temperature.

12oz fresh mackerel fillet (if unavailable, use salmon) *skinned and cut into large pieces*

¼ teaspoon ground turmeric

½ teaspoon ground cumin

½ teaspoon ground coriander

1-inch piece ginger root *peeled and finely grated*

1 teaspoon harissa

4 tablespoons virgin olive oil

1⅓ cups cold mashed potatoes (nothing added)

sea salt (or kosher salt) and freshly ground black pepper

for the coating

a little flour

1 egg *beaten*

1 cup fresh white bread crumbs

2½ tablespoons couscous

for the sauce

scant ½ cup mayonnaise

1 teaspoon harissa

1 teaspoon grated ginger root

tunisian fishcakes

The coating of the fishcakes in couscous gives an interesting texture to this dish. If mackerel is hard to find, use any firm, oily fish instead.

1 Place the mackerel pieces in a shallow dish. Add the spices, ginger, harissa, and half the olive oil. Mix well and lightly massage into the fish, then cover with plastic wrap and refrigerate for 4 hours.

2 Mix the sauce ingredients in a small bowl and refrigerate until needed.

3 Remove the fish from the marinade and place in a medium-size nonstick frying pan. Add a scant ½ cup water, cover, and cook for 3–4 minutes over a low heat, until tender. Remove and dry off any excess liquid. Let cool a little, then flake into a bowl.

4 When the fish is cold, add the mashed potato and mix thoroughly together. Season to taste. Divide the mixture into eight equal portions and roll into balls.

5 Dip the balls in a little flour, then in the beaten egg, and finally in the mixed bread crumbs and couscous. Flatten them slightly, then cook in the remaining olive oil in a nonstick pan, until golden and crispy. Drain on paper towels and serve with the sauce on the side.

1 cup plain set yogurt
3 scallions *finely chopped*
2 small green chiles *seeded and finely chopped*
1 tablespoon white wine vinegar
2 garlic cloves *crushed*
sea salt (or kosher salt)
1 fresh pomegranate *cut in half and seeds removed*
2 tablespoons freshly chopped dill
2 tablespoons freshly chopped mint
a little virgin olive oil

labna with green chile and pomegranate

Labna, a lovely refreshing dip made from strained yogurt, is extremely popular in the Middle East. This recipe has great flavor, lots of color, and tastes good either chilled or at room temperature. It's a perfect dip for dunking Middle Eastern-style flatbreads into.

1 In a bowl, mix the yogurt with the scallions, chiles, vinegar, and garlic. Season with salt.

2 Transfer to a serving bowl and sprinkle with the pomegranate seeds, dill and mint. Drizzle the olive oil over it and serve with Middle Eastern-style flatbread, such as pita or *lavosh*.

pg tip Middle Eastern flatbreads are very easy to make at home, but they are also widely available to buy, too. *Khubz* and *lavosh* make a nice change from the ubiquitous pita, and can also serve as a wrap for all sorts of fillings.

14oz chicken thighs *skinned and boned*
8 bay leaves
8 large pitted green olives
2 tablespoons virgin olive oil
1oz preserved lemons *pith removed and finely chopped*
2 tablespoons freshly chopped cilantro

for the marinade
1 garlic clove *crushed*
3 tablespoons virgin olive oil
½ teaspoon ground cardamom
¼ teaspoon ground cinnamon
1-inch piece ginger root *peeled and grated*

persian chicken brochettes

Preserved (or salted) lemons, which are used extensively in North African cooking, are available in good delis. They add an unmistakable, salty citric taste to these marinated chicken skewers.

1 Mix the ingredients for the marinade together in a bowl, add the chicken thighs, cover, and refrigerate overnight. The next day, cut the chicken into bite-size pieces.

2 When ready to serve, brush a ridged grill pan with a little olive oil and put it on the heat. Place the chicken pieces on the hot pan and cook for about 5 minutes, until tender. Remove from the heat and keep warm.

3 While the pan is still hot, grill the bay leaves and the olives, the latter only lightly. Once all three ingredients are grilled, thread one of each onto eight wooden skewers: one chicken piece, one bay leaf and one olive, in that order.

4 Transfer to a serving dish, mix the preserved lemons and cilantro together and sprinkle them over the brochettes when ready to serve.

the spice route

Along the Spice Route, in India, Thailand, Malaysia, and Indonesia, bite-size foods are imbued with the tantalizing flavors and aromas of ginger, coriander, lemongrass, turmeric, and chile.

10oz raw jumbo shrimp *shelled and deveined*

½ teaspoon grated ginger root

⅛ teaspoon each: chili powder, turmeric and chaat masala (see page 148)

½ teaspoon mild curry powder

1 egg white

1 tablespoon chickpea flour (gram flour)

sea salt (or kosher salt) and freshly ground black pepper

4 slices thick white sliced bread *crusts removed*

vegetable oil *for deep-frying*

for the sambal

2 ripe plum tomatoes *chopped*

½ red onion *chopped*

2 tablespoons chopped cilantro

juice of 2 limes

1 teaspoon cumin seeds *toasted and crushed*

curried shrimp toasts with tomato sambal

A play on the traditional prawn toasts seen endlessly on Chinese menus in England, these have a more spicy Indian feel.

1 For the sambal, mix all the ingredients in a bowl, then set aside for 1 hour for the flavors to infuse.

2 Place the shrimp, ginger, spices, and egg white in the food processor and blend to a paste. Transfer to a bowl, fold in the chickpea flour, and season to taste.

3 Spread the shrimp mixture on the slices of bread, ensuring an even coating.

4 Heat the oil to 325°F in a deep frying pan and deep-fry the bread with the shrimp mixture face down for just 20 seconds, until golden and crisp, then flip the bread over to brown the other side. Drain on paper towels.

5 Cut the toasts into quarters and serve with the sambal.

1 large baking potato (about 12oz)

¾ cup canned corn *well drained*

1 tablespoon chickpea flour (gram flour)

3 tablespoons vegetable oil

2 green chiles *seeded and finely chopped*

2 scallions *finely chopped*

½ teaspoon ground cumin

½ teaspoon ground coriander

2 tablespoons freshly chopped cilantro

sea salt (or kosher salt) and freshly ground black pepper

aloo corn tikki

One of India's culinary glories is its comforting street food, sold on every corner. These potato patties are one such street delicacy. Tamarind chutney makes a good accompaniment.

1 Preheat the oven to 350°F.

2 Place the potato on a baking tray in the oven and bake for 1 hour and 15 minutes. When cooked, remove and let cool.

3 Peel the potato, then place in a bowl and crush lightly. Add the corn and chickpea flour.

4 Heat 1 tablespoon of the oil in a small frying pan, add the chiles, scallions, and spices, and cook for 30 seconds. Add this to the potato and mix well. Add the chopped cilantro and season with salt and pepper.

5 Divide the potato mixture into equal-size balls, then shape into small patties. Heat the remaining oil in a frying pan, add the patties, and fry until golden and crisp.

1 teaspoon ground cumin

1 teaspoon coriander seeds *crushed*

½ teaspoon garlic salt

1 tablespoon paprika

1 teaspoon red pepper flakes

1 teaspoon ground ginger

2 teaspoons sea salt (or kosher salt)

4 x 4-oz salmon fillets *skinned and boned*

vegetable oil

lime slices *for garnishing*

bengali blackened salmon

The process of "blackening" food—quick searing in spices to produce a blackened crust—is traditionally a preparation used in Cajun cooking. Here's my fusion-style variation from farther east. The salmon looks great served on a banana leaf, and tastes good with mint- or tamarind-flavored yogurt.

1 Mix together all the spices and the salt, then use to rub into both sides of the salmon pieces. Place the fish on a tray, cover, and leave at room temperature for 30 minutes.

2 When ready to serve, heat up a frying pan over a high heat. Add a little oil to the pan, then cook the fillets for 2 minutes without moving them. Turn the fish over, cover, and cook for another 2 minutes. While the exterior should look blackened, the fish should be lightly cooked inside.

3 Serve garnished with some thin slices of lime.

10oz firm white fish fillet (e.g. sole, haddock, or halibut) *boned and skinned*

6 tablespoons chickpea flour (gram flour)

1 red onion *finely chopped*

2 scallions *finely chopped*

2 green chiles *seeded and finely chopped*

1 tablespoon chopped cilantro

1 teaspoon ground cumin

pinch of baking soda

sea salt (or kosher salt) and freshly ground black pepper

vegetable oil *for deep-frying*

fish pakoras

Pakoras are simple Indian fritters that are made by binding pieces of fish, meat, or vegetable in a batter made of chickpea flour, then frying them until crisp.

1 Chop the fish coarsely and place in a bowl. Stir in the flour and just enough water to make a thick batter coating around the fish. Add the remaining ingredients, excluding the oil.

2 Heat about an inch of the oil to 325°F in a deep frying pan. Using a spoon, drop equal amounts of the batter into the hot oil, in batches, and cook for 3–4 minutes or until the pakoras are cooked and crispy golden. Drain on paper towels.

1 large red chile *finely chopped*
2 garlic cloves *crushed*
²/₃ cup cashews *chopped*
1 tablespoon sesame oil
2 tablespoons chopped cilantro leaves
2 tablespoons tomato ketchup
½ teaspoon sugar
1lb swordfish fillet *boneless*
juice of 2 limes
sea salt (or kosher salt)
2 sheets banana leaf
a little oil *for greasing*

spicy sambal fish in banana leaf

You could replace the swordfish with fresh tuna in this recipe if you wish. Either way, serve the fish still in its banana leaf for an eye-catching presentation.

1 To make the spice paste, place the chile, garlic, nuts, and sesame oil in a mortar, or small blender, and grind or blitz to a coarse pulp. Transfer the mixture to a bowl, add the cilantro, ketchup, and sugar, and mix well. Set aside.
2 Cut the swordfish into four equal-size pieces and place in a dish. Squeeze the lime juice over them, season with salt, then cover and let marinate at room temperature for 30 minutes.
3 Remove the swordfish from the marinade, dry it well, then rub the spice paste onto both sides of the fish.
4 Soften the banana leaves by dipping them in very hot water until they become pliant. This takes about 30 seconds. Dry the leaves, then grease with a little oil. Place a piece of fish in the center of each leaf, then fold the edges up to form a purse, securing the top with raffia, kitchen string, a toothpick, or even a skewer.
5 Steam the wrapped fish in a steamer over simmering water, covered, for 8–10 minutes or until cooked through.

2 tablespoons vegetable oil
1 small onion *finely chopped*
¼ teaspoon ground turmeric
1 tablespoon curry powder
¼ teaspoon chili powder
½ pound (about 1 cup) ground lamb
sea salt (or kosher salt) and freshly
  ground pepper
1 tablespoon chopped mint
scant ½ cup sharp cheddar cheese,
  grated
1 egg *beaten*
4 nan breads

filled indian nans

These nan breads, filled with a spicy, cheesy lamb mixture, are satisfying to make and even more satisfying to unwrap when cooked.

1 Preheat the oven to 350°F.
2 Heat the oil in a large frying pan. When hot, add the onion and ground spices, and cook for 2–3 minutes to infuse the flavors.
3 Add the ground lamb and fry until the meat is sealed all over, cooked through, and almost dry in texture. Remove from the heat and let cool.
4 Season the cooled lamb to taste, add the mint and cheese, then bind with the egg. Spread this mixture on two of the nan breads, then top each one with a second nan, pressing down well to compact the filling.
5 Wrap each stuffed nan in foil, ensuring that they are fairly tightly wrapped. Place on a baking sheet in the oven for 10–12 minutes.
6 Let the filled nan cool slightly before serving, cut into strips.

1½ cups mashed potato

2 tablespoons chopped cilantro leaves

1 tablespoon chopped fresh mint leaves

1 red chile *seeded and finely chopped*

1 garlic clove *crushed*

4oz paneer cheese *coarsely grated*

sea salt (or kosher salt) and freshly
  ground black pepper

juice of ½ lemon

½ cup chickpea flour (gram flour)

pinch of baking powder

pinch of chili powder

vegetable oil *for deep-frying*

potato bonda

This classic Indian potato dish is easy to prepare and extremely good to eat.
You should be able to find paneer cheese, an Indian curd cheese, in an Indian
grocery store.

1 In a bowl, mix the mashed potato with the herbs, chile, garlic, and grated
  paneer cheese. Add the lemon juice and season with salt and pepper. Shape the
  mixture into walnut-size balls in the palm of your hands.

2 Mix the chickpea flour and baking powder together in a bowl, and season with
  salt and chili powder. Add enough water to form a thickish batter.

3 Heat the vegetable oil in a frying pan to 325°F.

4 Dip the potato balls in the batter, ensuring that they are completely coated, then
  drop them into the hot oil. Fry for 1–2 minutes, until golden.

5 Drain on paper towels.

pg tip A dip made of mint-flavored yogurt sweetened with a touch of honey
makes a great accompaniment to this dish.

1 cup ground beef

2/3 cup ground lamb

1 small onion *finely chopped*

1 garlic clove *crushed*

½ teaspoon ground ginger

½ teaspoon ground cumin

1 teaspoon ground cardamom

1/3 cup pitted dates *chopped*

2 tablespoons chopped fresh mint

sea salt (or kosher salt) and freshly
  ground black pepper

2 eggs

3 teaspoons rose water

2 tablespoons vegetable oil

meatballs with dates and rose water

Rose water is used extensively in Southern Indian cuisine, primarily in sweet
dishes. It has a very distinct flavor and perfume, and gives a distinctly exotic
touch to these meatballs.

1 In a large bowl, mix together the two meats, onion, garlic, spices, dates, and
  mint. Season with salt and pepper.

2 Work the meat together, add the eggs, and work again until thoroughly
  mixed. Add the rose water and let everything infuse for 30 minutes at room
  temperature.

3 Using wet hands, shape the mixture into small meatballs, then lightly
  flatten them.

4 Heat the oil in a frying pan, then fry the meatballs for 3–4 minutes, turning
  them once.

1 **garlic clove** *crushed*
1 **red chile** *finely chopped*
¾-inch piece ginger root *peeled and grated*
1 **shallot** *finely sliced*
1¼lb medium-size clams
juice of 1 lime
2 **tablespoons** *nam pla* **(Thai fish sauce)**
1½ tablespoons unsalted butter *chilled and cut into small pieces*
2 **tablespoons roughly chopped cilantro**

thai-style clams

Clams are such a versatile shellfish as their texture makes them ideal for all manner of preparations, although this Oriental-style version is one of my particular favorites.

1 Place the garlic, chile, ginger, and shallot in a wide pan and place the clams on top. Add $2/3$ cup water, cover with a tight-fitting lid, and bring rapidly to a boil.

2 Cook for 2 minutes, shaking the pan regularly, until the clams open. Discard any clams that do not open.

3 Add the lime juice, fish sauce, and butter, and stir to combine. Transfer to a serving dish, including all the pan juices, and scatter the cilantro on top.

1 **tablespoon vegetable oil**
½ **onion** *finely chopped*
1-inch piece ginger root *peeled and grated*
3oz cooked potatoes *peeled and cut into small pieces*
pinch of turmeric
¼ **teaspoon chili powder**
2 **teaspoons mild curry powder**
10oz chicken breast *boned and skinned*
sea salt (or kosher salt) and freshly ground black pepper
pinch of sugar
12oz pie dough

chicken puffs

These puffs originated quite by accident, when I was asked by an Indian guest for a canapé made with spicy chicken. They remain a feature on my cocktail menu.

1 Heat the oil in a nonstick frying pan. Add the onion and ginger and fry until the onion turns light golden brown. Add the potatoes, turmeric, chili powder, and curry powder, and cook for another minute.

2 Cut the chicken into small pieces and add to the pan, along with 4 tablespoons of water. Cover with a lid and cook for 6–8 minutes, until the chicken is cooked and the mixture almost dry. Add some salt and pepper and a little sugar. Remove from the heat and let cool.

3 Roll out the dough to $1/8$-inch thick, then cut out circles using a 3-inch cookie cutter.

4 Spoon some of the chicken filling into the center of each dough circle, then fold the pastry dough over to form a crescent. Wet the edges slightly and crimp to seal. Place in the fridge to rest for 30 minutes.

5 These pastries can either be baked, for 20–25 minutes at 325°F, or deep-fried until golden and crisp. Serve warm.

2 cups fresh white bread crumbs

3 tablespoons freshly chopped cilantro

½ cup unsweetened dried coconut flakes

8 stalks fresh lemongrass

1lb white fish fillets (e.g. cod or halibut) *boned and skinned*

1 small red chile *seeded and finely chopped*

2 tablespoons light soy sauce

2 scallions *finely chopped*

3 eggs

2 teaspoons cornstarch

zest of 1 lime

a little flour *for dipping*

4 tablespoons vegetable oil *for frying*

for the mayonnaise

3 tablespoons mayonnaise

splash of lime juice *to taste*

dash of chili oil

¼-inch piece ginger root *peeled and grated*

lemongrass fishcake skewers with lime-spiked mayonnaise

In this recipe, the lemongrass acts not only as a skewer, but also adds flavor. All you need to complement the fishcakes is the Asian-inspired mayonnaise and a nice crisp salad.

1 In a bowl, mix together the bread crumbs, cilantro, and coconut flakes, and set aside.

2 Clean the lemongrass and remove the tough outer casing. Finely chop two of the stalks, leaving the other six intact.

3 Cut the fish pieces into large chunks and put them in a blender. Add the chopped lemongrass, chile, soy sauce, scallions, and two of the eggs. Blitz the mixture for 20–30 seconds, until you have a smooth paste.

4 Spoon the fish mixture into a bowl, stir in the cornstarch and lime zest, then divide into twelve evenly sized balls. Shape the balls into round, flat patties, then dip them, one at a time, in a little flour, one at a time, the remaining egg (beaten), and finally into the coconut, cilantro, and bread crumb mixture.

5 Carefully thread two fishcakes onto each remaining lemongrass stalk; you may need to mold them on to make sure they are secure. Heat the oil in a large frying pan, then add the fish skewers and cook for 2 minutes on each side, until golden and crispy.

6 Drain the fishcakes on paper towels, then serve with the mayonnaise, made by simply mixing all the ingredients together.

14oz firm white fish fillets (e.g. monkfish (angler fish), sole, or halibut)

vegetable oil *for deep-frying*

4 kaffir lime leaves *shredded*

3 scallions *thinly shredded*

for the sauce

2 tablespoons red curry paste

½ cup coconut milk

1 teaspoon *nam pla* (Thai fish sauce)

1 teaspoon sugar

1 teaspoon dried shrimp paste

crispy fish in red curry

In Thailand they prepare this dish using a local fish, called *pla chron*, which is similar to mackerel. Personally, I prefer to use a firm-textured white fish.

1 First make the sauce. Mix the curry paste with the coconut milk, place in a pan, and cook gently for 4–5 minutes, until the sauce thickens.

2 Add the fish sauce, sugar and shrimp paste. Heat through, then set aside.

3 Cut the fish into bite-size pieces and fry in hot oil until crisp and golden. Drain on paper towels.

4 Place the crispy fish in a dish, pour the curry sauce over it, and garnish with the shredded lime leaves and scallions.

2 shallots *peeled*
4 garlic cloves *peeled*
1-inch piece ginger root *peeled and grated*
2 green chiles *seeded*
1 teaspoon Chinese five-spice powder
2 tablespoons hoisin sauce
1 tablespoon sesame oil
14oz chicken thighs *skinned and boned*
8 screwpine leaves *washed and dried*
vegetable oil *for deep-frying*

sweet chicken wrapped in screwpine leaves

Screwpine leaves (also known as pandanus leaves) grow profusely in Thailand where they are known as *pandan*. They are available dried and sometimes fresh from Asian markets and when used as a wrapper for chicken or fish, they impart a wonderfully earthy and exotic flavor during cooking.

1 Using a mortar and pestle, grind the shallots, garlic, ginger, and chiles to a coarse paste. Add the five-spice powder, hoisin, and sesame oil, and mix well.
2 Transfer to a bowl, add the chicken thighs, and rub the paste thoroughly into the meat. Let it marinate for 4 hours.
3 Wrap each chicken thigh in a screwpine leaf, as though you were wrapping a package, and use a toothpick to secure it.
4 In a deep pan, heat the vegetable oil to 325°F. Immerse the leaves in the hot oil and cook for 5–6 minutes.
5 Serve each screwpine wrap on an individual plate, allowing each diner to unwrap their own leaves.

8 small lambchops
2 green chiles
2 garlic cloves *crushed*
¾-inch piece ginger root *peeled and grated*
handful of cilantro *leaves only*
1 teaspoon plain yogurt
juice of 1 lemon
sea salt (or kosher salt)

lambchops in green masala

The green masala curry paste used in this recipe is a great base for chicken and lamb dishes. Dried coconut can be added to the paste, and the result is equally delicious.

1 Trim the chops free of all fat and clean the bones thoroughly.
2 Place the chiles, garlic, ginger, and cilantro in a blender, along with the yogurt and one quarter of the lemon juice, and blitz to a smooth paste.
3 Rub the paste over the chops, place them in a dish, cover with plastic wrap, and refrigerate overnight.
4 When ready to serve, heat a grill pan until almost smoking. Sprinkle the chops with salt and cook on the grill for 2–3 minutes, or until charred all over.
5 Arrange the chops on serving dishes, squeeze the remaining lemon juice over them, and serve.

12 **fresh scallops** *cleaned, on the half shell*

sea salt (or kosher salt) and freshly ground black pepper

1 **tablespoon mild curry powder**

2 **tablespoons unsalted butter**

for the relish

2 **tablespoons virgin olive oil**

1 **onion** *finely chopped*

2 **garlic cloves** *crushed*

1 **small green chile** *seeded and finely chopped*

1-**inch piece ginger root** *peeled and finely grated*

2 **tablespoons** *nam pla* **(Thai fish sauce)**

zest and juice of 4 limes (plus extra lime wedges for garnishing)

sea salt (or kosher salt) and freshly ground black pepper

2 **tablespoons freshly chopped cilantro**

broiled scallops with cilantro and lime relish

Grilling scallops brings out their natural sweetness to great effect, and the spicy lime relish acts as the perfect foil. This recipe is a big favorite with my family.

1 First, make the relish. Heat the olive oil in a pan, add the onion, garlic, chile, and ginger, and cook over a low heat until softened.

2 Add the fish sauce and lime zest and juice, along with a little seasoning. Cook over a low heat, until the mixture is very soft and aromatic. This will take about 15 minutes. Add the cilantro and cook for another 5 minutes. Transfer to a bowl and let cool.

3 Preheat the broiler to its highest setting.

4 Season each scallop liberally with salt, then sprinkle on a little pepper on them and dust with curry powder.

5 Place a good spoonful of relish in the bottom of each of the scallop shells. Top with a scallop, followed by a pat of butter. Place on a large baking sheet.

6 When the broiler is hot, pop the scallops under for 2–3 minutes or until just cooked. (Do not overcook the scallops as they will become tough.) Transfer the scallops to a dish and garnish with the lime wedges.

12 **large raw shrimp** *peeled, leaving the head and tail intact*

1 **tablespoon vegetable oil**

1 **garlic glove** *crushed*

10 **curry leaves**

2 **teaspoons unsalted butter**

pinch of sea salt (or kosher salt)

1 **large red chile** *chopped*

4oz **unsweetened dried coconut**

1 **teaspoon soy sauce**

1 **teaspoon red wine vinegar**

chile shrimp with curry leaf and coconut

Curry leaves have a pronounced flavor that goes fantastically with coconut and chile. They are available fresh from many Indian markets.

1 First, you need to devein the shrimp (see tip). Then wash and dry them, and place in a bowl. Add the oil, garlic, and curry leaves, and set aside for 20–30 minutes.

2 Heat a wok until almost smoking. Throw in the shrimp in their marinade and toss them, adding the sea salt and butter.

3 Add the remaining ingredients and stir-fry briskly for 2–3 minutes. Remove from the heat and serve immediately.

pg tip The black "vein" running down the back of the shrimp is the intestinal tract. It is not harmful if eaten, but the shrimp looks better without it. Using a small, sharp knife, simply make a shallow incision along the back of the shrimp, then carefully remove any black vein with the tip of the knife.

1 handful mint leaves *freshly chopped*
1 red chile *seeded and finely chopped*
½ teaspoon chaat masala (see pg tip below)
¼ teaspoon chili powder
¼ teaspoon turmeric
zest and juice of 1 lemon
1 tablespoon brown sugar
2 tablespoons plain yogurt
6oz paneer cheese *cut into 8 large sticks*
4 large red peppers
2 tablespoons virgin olive oil

spicy paneer-baked peppers with lemon and chile

I love the versatility of paneer cheese. I often use it in curries, or grill it (after marinating) in tandoori or tikka spices. It's also great wrapped in pita bread as part of a veggie sandwich. Basically, paneer is an all-round excellent cheese that doesn't melt or lose its shape when heated, and is available from Indian grocery stores.

1 In a bowl, mix together the mint, chile, chaat masala, chili powder, turmeric, lemon juice and zest, brown sugar, and yogurt. Add the cheese, cover with plastic wrap, and let marinate overnight in the fridge.

2 The following day, preheat the oven to 400°F.

3 Lay out a large sheet of foil on the counter, place the peppers in the middle, and drizzle a little olive oil over them. Scrunch up the foil to secure the peppers within, place on a baking tray, and roast in the oven for about 25 minutes. They should be soft but not overcooked. Remove and let cool.

4 Cut the cold peppers in half vertically, and remove the inner seeds. Place a stick of marinated cheese in each pepper and roll it to secure the cheese inside. Secure with a toothpick, then lightly flatten with the palm of your hand.

5 Place the rolled peppers on the baking tray, drizzle the remaining oil over them, and bake in the oven for 10 minutes, or until the pepper begins to char and the cheese softens.

6 Remove the toothpicks before serving.

pg tip Chaat masala, available ready-made in Indian grocery stores, is a spice mixture consisting of dried mango powder, cumin, black salt, coriander, dried ginger, and red pepper. Normally added to dishes at the end of cooking, it offers a pungent smell and a sweet-sour flavor.

1 medium onion *chopped*

1-inch piece ginger root *peeled and grated*

2 garlic cloves *crushed*

2 red chiles *finely chopped*

6 tablespoons virgin olive oil

1 tablespoon mild curry powder

½ teaspoon garam masala

²/₃ cup coconut milk

12 large raw shrimp *peeled and deveined*

12 small pitted black olives

2 tablespoons freshly chopped cilantro

stir-fried shrimp with olives and cilantro

The addition of olives to a spicy dish may seem unusual, but their saltiness really accentuates the flavors here. It is fun to eat this dish using fingers of nan or paratha bread to wrap the shrimp in.

1 Place half of the onion, and all of the ginger, garlic, and chiles in a small blender or food processor, and puree to a paste.

2 Heat half the olive oil in a large frying pan or wok. Add the paste and stir-fry over a medium heat, until the paste browns slightly and becomes aromatic.

3 Mix the curry powder and garam masala with 2 tablespoons of water, add this to the pan, and cook for 3–4 minutes. Add the coconut milk and simmer for another 5 minutes.

4 Heat the remaining oil in another frying pan or wok. Add the remaining onion and fry for 3–4 minutes. Throw in the shrimp and cook for 2 minutes, or until they turn red in color.

5 Pour the spicy sauce over them, add the olives and cilantro, and mix well together. Transfer to a dish and serve piping hot.

1 tablespoon tikka paste

1 tablespoon plain yogurt

½ teaspoon ground cumin

½ teaspoon ground cardamom

1 tablespoon chopped cilantro

¾-inch piece ginger root *peeled and grated*

1 garlic clove *crushed*

14oz ground chicken breast

a little oil

4 small nan breads

for the mint chutney

1 small bunch fresh mint

¾-inch piece ginger root *peeled and grated*

1 small green chile *chopped*

juice of ½ lime

½ teaspoon sugar

1 teaspoon ground coriander

1 small onion, *peeled and finely chopped*

a little plain yogurt *for blending* (water is fine, too)

sea salt (or kosher salt) and freshly ground black pepper

mini chicken tikka burgers with mint chutney

Burgers never lose their popularity, and these mini ones are always a talking point when I serve them. The mint chutney adds a nice Indian touch to the dish.

1 Place all the ingredients for the burgers (excluding the oil and nan breads) in a bowl and mix well. With wet hands, mold the mixture into twelve small burgers. Place these on a plate and refrigerate for 1 hour.

2 Meanwhile, make the chutney by placing all the chutney ingredients in a blender with enough yogurt or water to blitz to a thick sauce consistency. Season to taste.

3 Preheat a grill pan, then cook the burgers (brushed with a little oil) for 3–4 minutes on each side, until cooked through.

4 Meanwhile, cut each nan bread into three wedges, and toast until crispy. Top each nan wedge with a cooked burger and spear with a skewer.

pg tip Tikka paste is an Indian spice paste made from cumin and coriander seed, ginger, garlic, chile, and garam masala. If you don't have any to hand, a curry paste could be used as a substitute.

the far east

In dim sum and sushi, China and Japan offer mystical little packages of deliciousness that are perfect to share. They are packed with aromatic and flavorful combinations to tantalize your tastebuds and leave you wanting more.

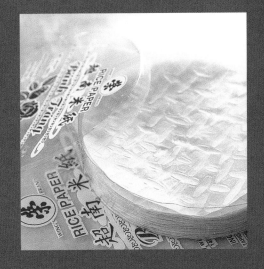

2 tablespoons white miso

1 tablespoon dark brown sugar

2 tablespoons sake

1 tablespoon mirin

1 egg yolk

1lb monkfish (angler fish) fillet *cleaned and cut into ¾-inch cubes*

1 teaspoon black sesame seeds

1 tablespoon vegetable oil

miso-glazed monkfish skewers

Miso, made by fermenting a mixture of soybeans, rice, and cereal grains, is a thick paste used in Japan to flavor soups and sauces, season grilled foods, or to pickle vegetables, meat, and fish. The two main types are red (strong and salty) and white (sweeter and milder in flavor).

Note: This recipe requires overnight marinating.

1 Mix the miso, brown sugar, sake, and mirin in a pan, then slowly bring to a boil. Reduce the heat and cook for 2–3 minutes, stirring occasionally. Add the egg yolk (this will immediately due to the heat), then transfer to a shallow dish and let cool.

2 Add the monkfish cubes, mix well with the marinade, then cover with plastic wrap and refrigerate overnight.

3 When ready to serve, thread the monkfish cubes onto small metal or presoaked wooden skewers, and sprinkle with black sesame seeds.

4 Brush a ridged grill pan with oil and place over the heat. When very hot, place the skewers on the pan and cook for 5–6 minutes, turning them regularly and basting them with the marinade. Serve hot from the grill.

oriental oyster shooters

1 cup tomato juice
¼ cup vodka
1 teaspoon wasabi paste
1 teaspoon mirin
½ teaspoon soy sauce
juice of 2 limes
1 teaspoon superfine sugar
sea salt (or kosher salt) and freshly
  ground black pepper
8 very fresh oysters *shucked and cleaned*
1 lime *for garnishing*

I can never get enough of these little shooters. Created from a classic bloody mary shooter, they are packed with Asian flavor and, for me, are better than the original.

1 In a bowl, mix together all the ingredients except the oysters and lime, and season to taste. Refrigerate for 1 hour for the flavors to meld together.
2 To serve, place 2 oysters each in the bottom of four small shot glasses, then pour the shooter mixture over them.
3 Garnish the glasses with lime wedges and serve chilled, with some chopsticks for digging out the oysters.

yakitori duck

3 tablespoons sake
¼ cup mirin
2 tablespoons sugar
¼ cup dark soy sauce
2 large duck breasts *skinned and boned*
5oz (about 1½ cups) small shiitake
  mushrooms *stalks removed*
2 tablespoons vegetable oil

Traditionally, *yakitori* (Japanese-style skewers) are made with chicken, but duck, and even pork and beef, are also superb cooked in this way. The sauce used to coat the chicken is traditionally used over and over again so that the flavor is rich and full. The skewers taste best when barbecued, but you can also cook them on a grill pan or under a broiler.

1 Place the sake, mirin, sugar, and soy sauce in a pan, bring to a boil, and simmer until reduced in volume by a third.
2 Cut the duck breasts in half, lengthwise, then into large cubes, and place in a bowl. Pour the marinade over them, add the mushrooms, cover with plastic wrap, and let marinate for 1 hour.
3 Drain the meat and the mushrooms, then thread them alternately onto presoaked wooden or bamboo skewers.
4 Cook on a preheated grill pan, brushed with a little oil, and cook until the skewered duck is beautifully charred and glossy, about 4–5 minutes.

pg tip Rice wine is an essential ingredient in Japanese and Chinese cooking, and is particularly useful in marinades and glazes. Chinese Shaoxing wine is often confused with Japanese sake, but the latter is more delicate in taste. Mirin, also from Japan, is essentially a sweetened sake. All three should be widely available, but if you can't find mirin you can use 2 parts dry sherry and 1 part sugar as a substitute.

¼ **English cucumber**
1 **bunch watercress**
4oz **(about 1 cup) cooked egg noodles**
4 **scallions** *finely sliced*
½ **small cooked Chinese BBQ duck**
  (available from Oriental stores)

for the dressing
2 **stalks lemongrass** *very finely chopped*
1 **tablespoon rice wine vinegar**
3 **tablespoons peanut or vegetable oil**
1 **small red chile** *finely chopped*
1-inch **piece ginger root** *peeled and*
  grated

chinese duck salad

It's amazing how such a tasty salad can be obtained from so few ingredients. Make sure you don't add the dressing until just before serving.

1 For the dressing, simply combine all the ingredients together in a bowl.
2 Cut the cucumber in half lengthwise, scoop out the seeds with a teaspoon, then slice into half moons. Combine with the watercress, noodles, and scallions in a large bowl.
3 Remove the skin from the Chinese duck and cut into thin shreds. Add to the bowl.
4 Pour the dressing over the salad and toss gently together. Divide into bowls and serve.

hot spare ribs

1¼lb pork spare ribs

2 large garlic cloves *crushed*

½ teaspoon ground cumin

1 teaspoon chili powder

1 teaspoon sesame oil

2 tablespoons vegetable oil

1 cup chicken stock (or water)

1 tablespoon maple syrup

2 tablespoons dark soy sauce

4 tablespoons *char siu* (Chinese BBQ sauce—see pg tip below)

Spare ribs, the most expensive cut of pork (from the lower portion of the belly and breastbone), are used in a variety of cuisines, including, of course, Chinese. They are best eaten by hand, so diners can simply gnaw the meat off the bone.

Note: This recipe requires overnight marinating.

1 Cut the spare ribs into 2–3-inch lengths, then cut between each rib to separate them. Place in a shallow dish.

2 Mix the garlic, cumin, and chili powder together in a bowl, then rub liberally into the flesh of the ribs. Cover and refrigerate overnight.

3 The next day, preheat the oven to 325°F.

4 Heat both oils in a wok or large frying pan over a high heat, add the ribs, and fry until nicely browned all over. Add the remaining ingredients, then bring to a boil.

5 Transfer the spare ribs and the sauce to a large baking tray, ensuring that the ribs are in a single layer. Bake in the oven for 40–45 minutes, or until the ribs are cooked and dark in color, and the sauce all but evaporated. Let cool slightly before serving.

pg tip *Char siu* is available in Asian stores, but you can make a reasonable approximation of it by simply mixing honey and dark soy sauce with a small amount of ground ginger and garlic.

japanese-style ceviche

1lb very fresh salmon fillet *cleaned and skinned*

1-inch piece ginger root *peeled and finely grated*

1 garlic clove *crushed*

1 teaspoon sugar

⅛ teaspoon wasabi paste

½ teaspoon sea salt (or kosher salt)

2 tablespoons shoyu (Japanese soy sauce)

6½ tablespoons sake

1 tablespoons pickled ginger *finely chopped*

2 scallions *finely chopped*

½ teaspoon black sesame seeds (optional)

Japanese cuisine is, in my opinion, one of the finest in the world. Food is prepared fresh and pure, particularly where fish is concerned. In an effort to conform, make sure that your salmon is as fresh as possible.

1 Cut the salmon, across the fillet, into ⅛-inch-thick slices. Arrange in a single layer in the bottom of a shallow dish.

2 Place the grated ginger, garlic, sugar, wasabi, and sea salt in a mortar and crush to a paste. Add the Japanese soy sauce, sake, and pickled ginger, and stir well.

3 Pour the marinade over the salmon, cover with plastic wrap, and refrigerate for 1 hour prior to serving.

4 When ready to serve, transfer the salmon to a serving plate, pour the marinade over it, and sprinkle with the scallions and black sesame seeds, if using.

¾ cup chicken stock

1 cup coconut milk

2 tablespoons virgin olive oil

½ onion *finely chopped*

1 small garlic clove *crushed*

½ cup risotto rice (Arborio or Vialone Nano)

2 tablespoons chopped cilantro

4oz (about 1 cup) shiitake mushrooms *chopped*

2 scallions *chopped*

2 eggs *beaten*

⅔ cup panko (Japanese bread crumbs)

⅓ cup unsweetened dried coconut

vegetable oil *for deep-frying*

coconut shiitake risotto balls

The idea for this recipe arose out of Italy's famous rice balls (*suppli*), but I've played around with the flavors. So the rice is cooked in coconut milk and the balls are filled with shiitake mushrooms.

1 Combine the stock and coconut milk in a pan and bring to a boil. Maintain at a gentle simmer.

2 Heat 1 tablespoon of the olive oil in a heavy pan. Add the onion and garlic, and cook until the onion is softened. Add the rice and stir well.

3 Stir in the simmering stock a half-cup at a time, and wait until the liquid has been absorbed before adding more, as you would with a classic risotto. Cook until the rice is just tender and all the stock has been used and absorbed. The total cooking time will be 20–25 minutes. Stir in the cilantro, then let the risotto cool.

4 Heat the other tablespoon of oil in a frying pan. When hot, add the mushrooms and the scallions, and cook over a high heat for 2–3 minutes, until tender. Remove from the heat and let cool.

5 Divide the cold risotto into small, walnut-size balls, press some cooked mushroom and scallion into the center of each one, and roll to enclose.

6 Coat the risotto balls in beaten egg, then roll in a mixture of panko and dried coconut.

7 Fry in oil heated to 300°F, until golden, then drain on paper towels.

pg tip These risotto balls can be made in advance and frozen (unfried) for up to one month.

1 cup ground pork

1-inch piece ginger root *peeled and grated*

2 garlic cloves *crushed*

sea salt (or kosher salt) and freshly ground black pepper

4 water chestnuts (canned is fine) *chopped*

3 teaspoons freshly chopped cilantro

1 cup cooked rice (preferably basmati or jasmine)

1 tablespoon *nam pla* **(Thai fish sauce)**

1 Chinese cabbage (napa cabbage) *separated into leaves*

shanghai-style dolmades

Dolmades are a simple Greek dish of vine leaf rolls filled with savory rice. They always remind me of a dish I had in the Far East, and here is my adaptation of that recipe. The stuffed leaves taste delicious dipped into either a sweet chili sauce or a plum sauce spiked with Tabasco.

1 Mix the pork with the grated ginger and garlic, along with a liberal seasoning of salt and pepper. Add the chopped water chestnuts, cilantro, and rice, and season with the fish sauce.

2 Blanch the cabbage leaves in boiling, salted water for 2–3 minutes, then refresh in iced water. Remove and dry in a cloth.

3 Cut away 2 inches from the bottom of each cabbage leaf. Lay out eight of the larger leaves on a counter, veined side down. Place an equal amount of pork mixture near the bottom of each leaf, then roll it up, tucking in the sides halfway to completely secure the filling.

4 Steam the rolls in a bamboo-style steamer (or regular steamer pan) over boiling water for 45 minutes, or until the pork is cooked through. Transfer the dolmades to a serving dish and serve.

pg tip If you can't get hold of Chinese cabbage, you could use large bok choy leaves, blanched spinach leaves, or even normal cabbage leaves (cooked).

1 cup short grain sushi rice *rinsed thoroughly in cold water*

2 tablespoons rice wine vinegar

½ tablespoon sugar

1 teaspoon sea salt (or kosher salt)

black sesame seeds

nori (seaweed) squares *for serving (optional)*

for the filling

4oz very fresh tuna fillet *cut into ¼-inch cubes*

1 tablespoon pickled ginger *finely chopped*

2 scallions *finely chopped*

1 tablespoon nori (seaweed) flakes

½ teaspoon wasabi paste

inside-out sushi

In one of my mad moments, I decided to reverse the way that sushi is prepared, hence "inside-out sushi." I hope you agree that the result looks rather dainty.

1 Place the rice in a pan with 2 cups water and bring to a boil. Reduce the heat and cook for 15 minutes, or until just tender. Remove from the heat, cover with a lid, and let stand for another 15 minutes.

2 Transfer the rice to a bowl and add the vinegar, sugar, and the salt. Toss together then set aside for the rice to cool.

3 In another bowl, mix together the cubed tuna, ginger, scallions, and nori flakes. Add the wasabi and lightly bind everything together.

4 Using wet hands, roll tablespoons of cold rice lightly in the sesame seeds to form small balls. Make a deep indentation in each ball with your finger and push a teaspoon of the tuna mixture into the center of the rice. Re-form the ball around it.

5 Arrange the stuffed rice balls on squares of nori seaweed (if using), or simply in a deep bowl, and serve at room temperature.

1 ripe avocado (preferably Hass variety)
1 teaspoon pickled ginger *finely chopped*
½ teaspoon wasabi paste
2 scallions *finely chopped*
juice of 2 limes
2 tablespoons crème fraîche
2 small fresh lotus root
vegetable oil *for deep-frying*

asian guacamole

Everyone loves guacamole, the classic Mexican dip. My variation comes from farther away, with the addition of flavors of the Orient. The lotus root (available in good Asian food stores) makes a great accompaniment, but wonton dipper chips (see page 170) would work well, too.

1 Cut the avocado in half, remove the pit and set it aside. Scoop out the flesh into a bowl and mash coarsely with a fork.

2 In another bowl, combine the remaining ingredients and stir gently into the mashed avocado.

3 If not eating the guacamole right away, you can refrigerate it for up to an hour. If doing so, place the reserved avocado pit in the guacamole (which will stop it turning black), cover with plastic wrap, and refrigerate.

4 Peel the lotus root and and then slice into $1/8$-inch-thick slices using a sharp knife or mandoline. Heat the oil to 325°F and deep-fry the root for about 1 minute, until golden and crispy. Drain on paper towels and cool before serving with the guacamole.

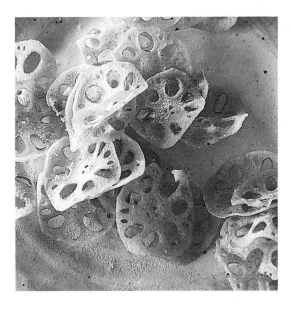

½ avocado *peeled and pitted*

⅛ teaspoon wasabi paste

2 tablespoons good-quality mayonnaise

¾-inch piece ginger root *peeled and grated*

1 tablespoon yuzu juice (or lime juice)

1 tablespoon tomato ketchup

⅔ cup fresh crabmeat

sea salt (or kosher salt) and freshly ground black pepper

trimmed mustard cress leaves (or alfalfa sprouts or other sprout leaves) and salmon caviar *for serving*

yuzu crab cocktail

Yuzu is a popular Japanese citrus fruit, a cross between a lime and a tangerine. It has a superb flavor and tastes wonderful in dressings, salsas, and sauces. Good Japanese markets should sell it, otherwise use lime.

1 Place the avocado and wasabi in a small bowl, and mash to a paste. Place to one side.

2 Combine the mayonnaise, ginger, yuzu (or lime) juice, and ketchup to form a sauce. Add the crabmeat and season to taste.

3 To serve, place a spoonful of the mashed avocado in the bottom of four small cocktail-style martini glasses. Top each with the crab mixture, and garnish with the cress leaves and salmon caviar.

pg tip Wonton chips make a nice and simple accompaniment to the yuzu crab cocktail. Simply cut the wonton skins in half diagonally, then fry in hot oil at 350°F, until golden and crispy. Drain on paper towels.

asian pesto-grilled chicken

This is a simple dish to prepare and delicious to eat. It's also a good way to use up the underfillet of the chicken breast.

1¼lb chicken breast fillets *boned and skinned*

sea salt (or kosher salt) and freshly ground black pepper

2 tablespoons chopped mint leaves

3 tablespoons chopped cilantro leaves

2 garlic cloves *crushed*

⅓ cup roasted peanuts

1¼-inch piece ginger root *peeled and grated*

pinch of sugar

¼ cup vegetable oil

extra vegetable oil *for frying*

scallions *thinly sliced, for serving*

1 Cut the chicken fillets into thick strips, then thread them lengthwise (satay-style) onto presoaked wooden or bamboo skewers. Place in a shallow dish and season with salt and pepper.

2 Combine the remaining ingredients in a blender and mix to a coarse pulp. Pour half over the chicken, cover with plastic wrap, and marinate for 2–3 hours in the fridge.

3 Brush a grill pan liberally with oil, then place over a high heat. When very hot, place the skewers on the pan and cook gently, turning them regularly, for 4–5 minutes.

4 Arrange the skewers on a dish, pour the remaining pesto over them, and scatter the scallions on top.

spiced salt and pepper tofu

If you love tofu, you'll love this recipe. Peanut sauce is my favorite accompaniment, but I occasionally like to serve this with an orange honey sauce (simply warmed honey with some fresh orange juice and zest added), or a spiced soy sauce.

3 x 4-oz firm tofu *cut into ¾-inch cubes*

1 teaspoon black peppercorns

2 teaspoons sea salt (or kosher salt)

¼ teaspoon Chinese five-spice powder

1 tablespoon flour (or cornstarch)

vegetable oil *for stir-frying*

for the peanut sauce

⅓ cup roasted peanuts *chopped*

1 tablespoon smooth peanut butter

1 teaspoon *nam pla* (Thai fish sauce)

⅓ cup sweet chili sauce

1 To make the peanut sauce, put all the sauce ingredients in a pan, together with 2 tablespoons of water, and heat gently until amalgamated.

2 Place the cubes of tofu between two layers of paper towels for about 30 minutes, to remove any excess water.

3 Meanwhile, heat a frying pan and dry fry the peppercorns for about 1 minute, until fragrant. Transfer to a mortar, add the salt and five spice, and crush to a fine powder.

4 Mix the spice mixture with the flour in a bowl and use this to coat the tofu cubes, shaking off any excess.

5 Heat a little oil in a wok. When hot, add the tofu cubes in batches and stir-fry until lightly golden. Drain on paper towels, then serve with the peanut sauce in a bowl alongside it.

7oz (about 1 cup) fresh raw peeled
  shrimp *finely chopped or ground*

1 tablespoon chopped fresh chives

2 scallions *very finely chopped*

1 carrot *peeled and finely chopped
  or grated*

2½ tablespoons cornstarch

1 teaspoon sea salt (or kosher salt)

1 teaspoon sesame oil

a pinch of sugar

6 medium-size fresh scallops

12 *gow gee* wrappers (wonton skins)

scallop shumai

For a change, feel free to replace the scallop filling for these Chinese dumplings with something else, such as a mixture of ground pork and shrimp or chicken. Always serve them with a dipping sauce, even if it's just soy sauce.

1 Place the shrimp, chives, scallions, and carrot in a bowl, along with the cornstarch. Add the salt, sesame oil and sugar and mix well. Cut the scallops into ½-inch pieces and add to the bowl.

2 Let it marinate, covered with plastic wrap, for 1 hour.

3 To make the dumplings, first cut the wrappers with a 2½–3-inch round cookie cutter.

Then, lay a circle in the palm of your hand and place a good spoonful of the shrimp and scallop mixture in the center. Bring up the sides of the wrapper to form a nice shape, keeping the top exposed. Prepare all twelve dumplings in the same way.

4 Steam the dumplings in a bamboo-style steamer, over a wok or pan of boiling water, for just 4–5 minutes, or until cooked. Alternatively, cook them gently in a pan of just simmering water.

scant cup flour

1 egg *beaten*

½ cup beer (any light beer)

12 large raw jumbo shrimp *shelled and
  deveined, tails intact*

1 cup unsweetened dried coconut

vegetable oil *for deep-frying*

for dipping sauce

3 tablespoons Chinese mustard (or
  Dijon mustard)

1 teaspoon lemon juice

2 tablespoons honey

1 tablespoon sweet chili sauce

beer-battered coconut shrimp

Thai coconut shrimp are delicious, simple to prepare, and quick to be eaten! The beer gives a lightness to the batter, while also adding a yeasty flavor.

1 Make a beer batter from the flour, egg, and beer, ensuring that it is nice and smooth.

2 For the sauce, mix all the ingredients together in a pan, then warm through until blended and smooth.

3 Heat the vegetable oil to 325°F.

4 Dip the shrimp in the prepared batter, roll it in the coconut, then deep-fry until golden. Drain on paper towels, then serve with the warm dipping sauce.

2 tablespoons sesame oil

9oz butternut squash *peeled and cut into ½-inch cubes*

1 onion *finely chopped*

1-inch piece ginger root *peeled and finely grated*

2 tablespoons freshly chopped cilantro

1 red chile *seeded and finely chopped*

4 tablespoons roasted cashews *chopped*

2 tablespoons hoisin sauce (plus extra for serving)

sea salt (or kosher salt) and freshly ground black pepper

12 spring roll wrappers

1 egg *beaten*

vegetable oil *for deep-frying*

hoisin sauce *for dipping*

butternut cashew pohpiahs

Traditionally, these spring rolls are made in Malaysia using a special *pohpiah* dough, a white sticky dough that is skillfully spread over a wok to give an almost translucent skin. You'll be pleased to hear that, for practicality's sake, in my recipe I have used spring roll wrappers, which are just as good.

1 Heat the sesame oil in a wok or frying pan, add the squash cubes and onion, and cook until they begin to soften.

2 Remove from the heat, add the ginger, cilantro, chile, and cashews, and stir-fry for 1 minute. Add the hoisin sauce, bind together, and season to taste.

3 Lay out one spring roll wrapper on the counter, then place a good spoonful of the filling in the center, leaving a good gap on each side. Brush the two long sides with egg and fold these over to meet in the center. Then roll the filled pastry tightly away from you, using more egg to hold the final closing join together. Prepare all the rolls in the same manner.

4 Heat the oil to 350°F, then deep-fry the spring rolls until golden and crispy. Drain well on paper towels.

5 Serve with hoisin sauce for dipping.

2 cooked smoked chicken breasts, skin on

2 tablespoons *kecap manis* (Indonesian soy sauce)

2 garlic cloves *crushed*

¾-inch piece ginger root *peeled and grated*

2 tablespoons cornstarch

½ teaspoon *sansho* pepper (or black pepper, cracked in a mortar)

sea salt (or kosher salt)

vegetable oil *for deep-frying*

lemon wedges *for serving*

eastern smoked chicken nuggets

Sansho pepper, used in the coating of these chicken nuggets, is the Japanese name for Szechuan pepper. It is one of the very few spices used in Japanese cooking and has a pungent, woody aroma and a peppery, slightly citrussy flavor. *Kecap manis* is a favorite Asian ingredient of mine. It has a hint of licorice which is excellent in this dish.

1 Cut the chicken breasts into 1-inch cubes and place in a shallow dish. Pour the Indonesian soy sauce over them, then add the garlic and ginger and rub liberally all over the chicken pieces. Cover with plastic wrap and refrigerate for 30 minutes.

2 Mix the cornstarch with the pepper and a little sea salt. Remove the chicken from the marinade and dip it in the cornstarch.

3 Heat the vegetable oil to 350°F. When hot, immerse the chicken pieces and fry quickly until golden and crispy.

4 Drain the chicken nuggets on paper towels, sprinkle with a little sea salt, and serve with lemon wedges.

2 tablespoons vegetable oil (plus extra
  for deep-frying)

2 scallions *finely chopped*

½ teaspoon ground coriander

5oz (about 1 cup) cooked new potatoes
  peeled

²/₃ cup unsweetened dried coconut

8 large jumbo shrimp *peeled and
  deveined, tail intact*

1 tablespoon fresh lime juice

2 teaspoons sesame seeds

8 x 6-inch round rice paper wrappers
  (plus extra in case of tearing)

1 egg white

vegetable oil *for deep-frying*

stuffed shrimp in rice skins

Rice papers are very thin, edible paper sheets made from parts of the rice plant.
Be patient cooking this recipe as the preparation is definitely fiddly, but worth
the effort. Sweet chili sauce with a dash of soy sauce added makes a good
dipping sauce for the shrimp.

1 Heat the oil in a wok or frying pan, add the scallions and coriander, and cook for
  30 seconds. Add the cooked potatoes, breaking them up into a rough mash, and
  fry together for 3–4 minutes.

2 Stir in the coconut, then remove the potato mixture to a bowl and let cool.

3 Toss the shrimp with the lime juice and sesame seeds, and let marinate for
  30 minutes.

4 When the shrimp is ready, use a small knife to cut along the back of each one,
  without cutting right through, to form a butterfly shape. Fill each shrimp with
  some filling, pressing the sides back carefully to close. Push a presoaked satay-
  size skewer through the bottom of each shrimp and out through the top: this will
  ensure that the shrimp keep their shape as they cook.

5 Immerse the rice paper wrappers in water, to soften them, and then dry with
  a clean, lint-free cloth. Brush each wrapper liberally with egg white and use to
  wrap the shrimp. Secure with a toothpick.

6 Deep-fry the shrimp in oil heated to 350°F, for 1–2 minutes, until golden and
  crispy. Drain on paper towels before serving.

8 eggs

4 tablespoons vegetable oil

3oz shiitake mushrooms *thinly sliced*

1 red chile *finely chopped*

½ cup fresh crabmeat

2 tablespoons roughly chopped
cilantro leaves

1 tablespoon soy sauce

for serving: 2 scallions and 1 banana
shallot (elongated in shape), both
thinly sliced, and some fresh
cilantro leaves

egg fu yung

This dish originated in the city of Shanghai, and was prepared with egg and chopped ham. Since the arrival of Chinese chefs in America, many variations have been created using vegetables and seafood.

1 Beat the eggs in a bowl until foamy.

2 Heat a wok or small nonstick frying pan. Add 2 tablespoons of the oil, then throw in the mushrooms and chile, and stir-fry for 1 minute. Add the crabmeat and cilantro and heat through. Pour the soy sauce over them and mix well together.

3 Pour the remaining oil around the side of the wok then pour it over the eggs. Cook over a medium heat, until the egg is lightly golden on the bottom, then flip the "omelette" over to cook the top. If you don't want to flip the omelette over, you can brown the top under a hot broiler.

4 Turn the fu yung onto a plate, sprinkle the sliced scallions and shallot on top, then scatter the whole cilantro leaves on top.

1½ cups flour

½ cup self-rising flour

4 tablespoons vegetable oil

4 scallions, green part only *finely chopped*

2 tablespoons sour cream

5oz smoked salmon (lox) slices

½ teaspoon wasabi paste

freshly ground black pepper

scallion pancakes with smoked salmon and wasabi

This recipe takes a common Chinese appetizer and makes it more lavish with the addition of smoked salmon, sour cream, and wasabi (hot Japanese horseradish).

1 Bring a scant cup of water to a boil. Sift the flours in a bowl, then gradually add them to the boiling water, mixing thoroughly all the time.

2 Add enough cold water to make a soft pliable dough, then knead this for 2–3 minutes. Return the dough to the bowl, cover with plastic wrap, and leave for 30 minutes at room temperature.

3 Divide the dough into two and roll out each half into two large circles, about ⅛-inch thick. Brush the surface with some of the vegetable oil, then sprinkle the scallions on top. Roll up each dough circle into a sausage shape, then cut each sausage into four sections. Re-roll each section into thick round pancakes.

4 Heat some more oil in a nonstick frying pan and fry each pancake for 1–2 minutes on each side, until golden.

5 Spread each pancake liberally with sour cream. Top this with smoked salmon, a dab of wasabi paste, and a twist of black pepper, then roll the pancake up.

6 Cut the pancake rolls into pieces before serving.

2 tablespoons peanut oil

2 garlic cloves *crushed*

4 scallions *finely chopped*

1 small red chile *seeded and finely chopped*

1-inch piece ginger root *peeled and grated*

1 small red pepper *seeded and finely chopped*

1 small green pepper *seeded and finely chopped*

2 tablespoons sake

1 tablespoon light soy sauce

2 tablespoons sweet chili sauce

2¼lb fresh mussels *scrubbed and debearded*

wok-roasted mussels

What I adore about mussels, apart from the taste, is the fact that they take no time to cook—a great dish in minutes. Using the wok for this recipe is ideal given the short cooking time.

1   Heat a wok or large frying pan, then add the oil, garlic, scallions, chile, and ginger, and stir-fry for 10 seconds.

2   Add the peppers, stir-fry for another 2 minutes, then pour in the sake, soy sauce, and chili sauce. Boil rapidly.

3   Throw in the mussels, cover with a lid, and cook for 2–3 minutes, or until the mussels have opened. (Discard any mussels that do not open.) Transfer to a deep serving bowl and serve immediately.

---

4 red snapper fillets *cleaned and scales removed (mackerel is good, too)*

2 teaspoons sea salt (or kosher salt)

1¼-inch piece ginger root *peeled and grated*

zest and juice of 1 lemon

4 tablespoons (¼ cup) sake

2 tablespoons virgin olive oil

steamed rice *for serving* **(optional)**

sea salt fish with sake and lemon

Japanese salt-grilled fish is one big treat for the taste buds. In Japan, the term *shioyaki* is used to describe the traditional method of salt-grilling beef, poultry, or, of course, fish. For me, the best cooking method of any salt-grilled food is quickly over hot coals.

1   Dry the fish fillets on paper towels, then make three diagonal slashes into the flesh of each one. Place in a shallow dish.

2   Mix together the salt, ginger, and zest and juice of the lemon in a bowl. Pour the mixture over the fish, then let this marinate, covered, in the fridge for 30 minutes.

3   Remove the fish from the fridge and sprinkle the sake over it, rubbing it liberally but carefully into the flesh.

4   Heat a grill pan until very hot. Brush the fish with olive oil, then place on the grill. Cook for 4–5 minutes, turning the fillets over once during cooking. (The cooking time is, of course, dependent upon the thickness of the fillets.)

5   Remove from the heat and serve immediately.

1/3oz dried wild mushrooms

6oz ground pork belly

5oz (about 2/3 cup) freshly picked
  crabmeat

1 egg *beaten*

3 tablespoons freshly chopped cilantro

1-inch piece ginger root *peeled and*
  finely grated

2 scallions *finely chopped*

1 garlic clove *crushed*

sea salt (or kosher salt)

3 sheets spring roll wrappers

a handful of chives (minimum 12)

vegetable oil *for deep-frying*

beggars' purses

These simple little Chinese pastry purses are filled with pork and crabmeat.
If spring roll pastry is not available, wonton skins or even phyllo pastry dough
would work okay.

1 Just cover the dried mushrooms in boiling water in a bowl, and soak for
  20 minutes. Drain and dry them thoroughly, then chop finely.

2 In a bowl, mix together the mushrooms, pork, crab, and beaten egg. Stir in
  the remaining ingredients (except the spring roll wrappers, chives, and oil) and
  combine well.

3 Cut each of the spring roll wrappers into four squares. Put the chives in hot
  water for 5 seconds to soften, as you'll need these for tying the "purses."

4 Place a little of the prepared filling in the center of each wrapper. Bring
  up the edges to form a topknot and tie tightly with the softened chives.

5 Heat the vegetable oil to 325°F, then cook the purses until crisp, golden brown,
  and cooked through. Remove with a slotted spoon and drain on paper towels.

pg tip These crispy purses are fantastic served with the following dipping sauce:
stir 1 tablespoon sugar into 4 tablespoons warm water. Add 3 tablespoons fish
sauce, and 2 tablespoons each of rice wine vinegar and lime juice. Finally, add
a clove of crushed garlic and a thinly sliced hot Thai chile. Let them infuse for
2 hours before using for the best results.

1 egg white

1 tablespoon cornstarch

2 tablespoons Shaoxing wine
  (or dry sherry)

1lb pork belly strips *cut into 1-inch*
  pieces

3 tablespoons peanut oil

1 garlic clove *crushed*

1-inch piece ginger root *peeled and*
  grated

2 scallions *thinly sliced*

2 red chiles *thinly sliced*

1/3 cup *char siu* (Chinese BBQ sauce)

2/3 cup chicken stock

1 teaspoon soy sauce

wok-fried bbq pork

Pork belly strips are great in stir-fries as opposed to tenderloin, which tends to
be dry. The natural fat in the belly keeps the meat deliciously juicy.

1 In a bowl, mix together the egg white, cornstarch, and wine. Add the pork pieces
  and mix well together.

2 Heat a wok or large frying pan with half the peanut oil. Throw in the pork and
  stir-fry for 3–4 minutes, until the meat is golden all over. Transfer to a dish.

3 Add the garlic, ginger, scallions, chiles, and remaining peanut oil to the wok and
  stir-fry for 1 minute. Add the barbecue sauce, stock, and soy sauce and cook for
  another minute.

4 Return the pork to the sauce, toss to coat, and reheat.

Weight (solids)

7g	¼oz
15g	½oz
20g	¾oz
25g	1oz
40g	1½oz
60g	2oz
70g	2½oz
85g	3oz
100g	3½oz
115g	4oz (¼lb)
125g	4½oz
140g	5oz
155g	5½oz
170g	6oz
200g	7oz
230g	8oz (½lb)
255g	9oz
285g	10oz
310g	11oz
340g	12oz (¾lb)
370g	13oz
400g	14oz
425g	15oz
455g	1lb
500g (½kg)	17½oz
600g	1¼lb
700g	1½lb
750g	1lb 10oz
900g	2lb
1kg	2¼lb
1.1kg	2½lb
1.2kg	2lb 12oz
1.3kg	3lb
1.5kg	3lb 5oz
1.6kg	3½lb
1.8kg	4lb
2kg	4½lb
2.25kg	5lb
2.5kg	5lb 8oz
3kg	6¾lb

Volume (liquids)

5ml	1 teaspoon
10ml	1 dessertspoon
15ml	1 tablespoon or ½fl oz
30ml	1fl oz
40ml	1½fl oz
60ml (¼ cup)	2fl oz
60ml	2½fl oz
90ml	3fl oz
100ml	3½fl oz
120ml (½ cup)	4fl oz
150ml	5fl oz
160ml	5½fl oz
180ml (¾ cup)	6fl oz
210ml	7fl oz
240ml (1 cup)	8fl oz
270ml	9fl oz
300ml (1¼ cups)	10fl oz
330ml	11fl oz
360ml (1½ cups)	12fl oz
380ml	13fl oz
410ml (1¾ cups)	14fl oz
440ml	15fl oz
470ml (2 cups)	16fl oz
530ml	18fl oz
550ml	19fl oz
590ml (2½ cups)	20fl oz
950ml	32fl oz (1 quart)
1.89 liters	64fl oz (½ gallon)
3.78 liters	128fl oz (1 US gallon)

Length

5mm	¼in
1cm	½in
2cm	¾in
2.5cm	1in
3cm	1¼in
4cm	1½in
5cm	2in
7.5cm	3in
10cm	4in
15cm	6in
17.5cm	7in
20cm	8in
25cm	10in
28cm	11in
30.5cm	12in

Oven temperatures

Celsius*/Fahrenheit   Gas/Description

110°C/225°F	mark ¼/cool
120°C/250°F	mark ½/cool
140°C/275°F	mark 1/very low
150°C/300°F	mark 2/very low
160°C/325°F	mark 3/low
180°C/350°F	mark 4/moderate
190°C/375°F	mark 5/mod. hot
200°C/400°F	mark 6/hot
220°C/425°F	mark 7/very hot
230°C/450°F	mark 8/very hot

*For fan-assisted ovens, reduce temperatures by at least 10°

acknowledgements Firstly I would like to thank my family for their understanding whilst I've been engrossed at weekends writing this book. *Thanks also go to:* Lara Mand who works wonders, deciphering my scrawls on paper and somehow translating them into order! Linda Tubby, good friend and home economist who knows me so well, and translates my ideas and recipes perfectly onto the plate. Pete Cassidy, for once again, some wonderful photography. Róisín Nield and Helen Trent for capturing the mood with their superb props. Jane Humphrey for laying out the pages so beautifully. Jane Middleton for her continued support and friendship on the project. Barry Tomkinson, one of my many young and talented chefs of the future, for his help with recipe testing and preparation. Friends Glenn Ewart of Churchill China PLC and Paul Goodfellow of Continental Chef Supplies for help with certain glassware and chinaware for the photography. A special thank you to Jennifer Wheatley, project editor and Emily Hatchwell, copy editor, for their enthusiasm and encouragement with my ideas. They both have been a real pleasure to work with.

photographic acknowledgements All photography by Peter Cassidy except for the following: page 4 and 70 Neil Emmerson / Getty Images; 10 Brand X Pictures / Alamy; 40 Andrea Pistolesi / Getty Images; 100 Stuart Westmorland / Getty Images; 130 Beth Callahan / Alamy; 154 Jeff Spielman / Getty Images